D0069196

WORKING ON YOURSELF DOESN'T WORK

A BOOK ABOUT
INSTANTANEOUS TRANSFORMATION®

ARIEL & SHYA KANE

ASK Productions, Inc.
New York
www.ask-inc.com

Working on Yourself Doesn't Work
A Book About Instantaneous Transformation®
Copyright © 1999 ASK Productions, Inc.
All rights reserved. Printed in the United States of America. No part
of this publication may be reproduced, stored in a retrieval system or
transmitted in any form or by any means, electronic, mechanical, pho-
tocopying, recording or otherwise without the written permission of
the publisher except by a reviewer who may quote brief passages in a
review.

Illustrations by Barnett Plotkin
Cover Design by Helene DeLillo
Cover Photo by Ariel Kane
Layout by Geert Teuwen
Kanes' Photo by Geert Teuwen

Library of Congress Catalogue Card Number: 99-90625

Kane, Ariel.
     Working on yourself doesn't work : a book about
instantaneous transformation / Ariel & Shya Kane.
-- 1st ed.
    p. cm.
    LCCN: 99-90625
    ISBN: 1-888043-04-0

    1. Self-actualization (Psychology)
2. Self-realization. 3. Satisfaction. 4. Happiness.
I. Kane, Shya. II. Title.

    BF637.S4K36 1999   158.1
                  QBI99-860
For information contact:
ASK Productions, Inc.
PMB 137
208 East 51st Street
New York, NY 10022-6500
     or
website address: http://www.ask-inc.com
email: kanes@ask-inc.com

Praise for Ariel & Shya Kane and "Working on Yourself Doesn't Work"

"My job is to provide people with information so they can have their lives work magically. I would be remiss if I didn't heartily recommend *Working on Yourself Doesn't Work*. Ariel and Shya Kane are at the forefront in the field of personal transformation and have much to offer anyone who wants a more meaningful and fulfilling life."

> *Paul English, Publisher, Managing Editor*
> *Free Spirit Magazine*
> *Southern California Spirit Magazine*

"As a physicist I don't know how they do it. But my life has transformed by being around the Kanes. When serious life events have come up — prostate cancer, my son disabled by a brain tumor, losing a job due to downsizing — I have been able to remain on-center and engaged in my life, not a victim."

> *William R. Ellis, Ph.D.*
> *Vice President, Advanced Technology*
> *Raytheon, a Fortune 500 Company*

"The Kanes create a miraculous space where I quit worrying. *Working on Yourself Doesn't Work* has allowed me to rediscover my passion for life and ability to have fun."

> *Ellen Jackson*
> *Loving Mother and Wife*

"In an era of technological revolutions affecting how we work and how we communicate, the Kanes are creating a revolution in how we live."

> *Andrew Gideon*
> *Vice President, TAG Online, Inc.*

"The Kanes - They gave me laughter
And also eyes to see.
If it's to be, it's up to me;
Awareness is the key."

> *Carol Oster Ellis, M.D.*
> *President*
> *New York Occupational Medical Association*

WHEN SHYA WAS LITTLE, HE ASKED HIS MOTHER, IDA,
WHY PEOPLE WERE SO UNHAPPY AND WHY THERE WAS
SO MUCH PAIN AND SUFFERING IN THE WORLD.

SHE REPLIED, "I DON'T KNOW.
IT HAS ALWAYS BEEN THIS WAY. WHEN YOU GROW UP,
MAYBE YOU CAN DO SOMETHING ABOUT IT."

THIS BOOK IS DEDICATED TO OUR PARENTS

GERI AND DON
MAX AND IDA

AND TO ALL THOSE WHO EVER DREAMT
OF MAKING A DIFFERENCE.

WHAT MAKES THIS BOOK
UNIQUE IS OUR BASIC PREMISE
THAT WORKING ON YOURSELF
DOESN'T WORK. ALL IT TAKES
TO HAVE YOUR LIFE TRANSFORM
IS GETTING INTO AND LIVING
FROM THE MOMENT -- THIS
CURRENT MOMENT OF NOW.

PREFACE

THIS BOOK WILL CLEAR A PATH THAT CAN EASE YOU INTO YOUR own Self-Discovery.

Having personally fallen into most of the pitfalls that keep one from being in the moment, we are experienced guides who have brought many people through the swamp of the mind into the clarity and brilliance of the moment.

In these pages, we will highlight not only those techniques and methods that you can use to unlock your true potential, but also we will outline the inhibitors to living your life directly. By living your life directly we mean that you will be empowered in your ability to experience life, take actions and be yourself rather than think about what to do next and worry whether or not you are doing your life the right way.

INTRODUCTION

COUNTLESS NUMBERS OF US HAVE DONE THERAPY OF
one sort or another. We have taken seminars on subjects ranging
from our wounded inner child to time management. We have
invested time and money in everything from meditation retreats
to walking on fire and high-energy effectiveness trainings. We
have planned our days, changed our diets and visualized our
goals.

And yet, for the two of us, after attending hundreds of
seminars and courses, and reading plenty of inspirational books,
there was still a sense of emptiness. After each seminar, retreat or
book, we would have a new system through which to view life.
We would feel hyped up or enthusiastic about ourselves, sometimes even changed and revitalized, but sooner or later, we would
be lying awake at night thinking, "There has got to be more to
life than this."

At first we could blame the emptiness on goals. We had not met our goals. But soon after we got the things we had been targeting -- the home on Park Avenue, the successful careers, not to mention loads of friends and a great relationship -- the emptiness, that feeling that we were missing something, got too strong to be ignored.

So we quit. We sold the Park Avenue apartment, had a New York City version of a garage sale and sold all of our things. We bought two backpacks, some supplies and set off to see the world. Actually we only got as far as Northern Italy. The beginning of our world tour included a stop at a meditation center where we had booked yet another three-week workshop. However, this time, something was different. When we got to this center, we stopped running: running from the emptiness -- running from ourselves.

We stayed there for the better part of two years, examining and questioning everything: our thoughts, our culture, our truth and even if we should continue being together. We participated in groups, many month-long, on healing, breath, dance, intuition, massage and an advanced counselor's training. The last workshop we did was a six-month long, 24 hour a day, meditation intensive.

At the end of these six months, it was the end of taking workshops. We said "Forget it! No more!" We were done trying to fix ourselves. (And very shortly thereafter trying to fix each other.) By now we had managed to spend almost all of the money we had gotten from the sale of the apartment. Our credit cards were maxed-out, but at least we still had each other and a newly found sense of ourselves. Landing back in the United States, we borrowed a car, went to San Francisco and rented a room.

It was around this time we started discovering that we were rich. Although we had very little in the way of money, we felt well in ourselves. We were in love. We felt fulfilled and even though we were not sure what we would do next in our lives, we were at peace. At night we were reading aloud to each other from a book called "The Unborn, the Life and Teaching of Zen Master Bankei" which is a book of a 17th century Zen master's dissertations and teachings on the subject of Self-Realization. Soon it became apparent to us that we were living consistent with the way of being described in this book.

It became apparent to our friends as well. People wanted to know what had happened. "You are so different," they said. Just being around us they felt centered and at peace with themselves. They invited us to speak with them and their friends ...our first workshops were born.

We were now embarking on a grand new adventure -- the adventure of a lifetime. We had to define and communicate the essence of how we lived and approached life. This was a challenge. How does one express what is inexpressible in words? Once we had begun living life with a moment-to-moment sense of well-being, we had forgotten that our state of being wasn't the norm. When we let go of the past, we quickly forgot all of the pain and striving that had been so much a part of our daily existence. Having gone through as much as we had in our lives, independently and together, we discovered we had a knack for being incredibly insightful. Now, when we see people in pain, vainly running down the fruitless roads that we have traveled, we can say, "We know you. We have been there. It doesn't have to take as long for you as it did for us. You can get here today, now, this instant." And it's true. Through our Instantaneous Transformation® technology, many people are finding their true selves quickly now. It's exciting. We have seen over and over, regardless of age, race, sex, nationality or religion, people's lives transform -- instantaneously. You don't need to work on yourself. Just getting to this moment is enough.

This book can facilitate personal, individual transformation. By presenting a blend of our ideas and personal experiences we have addressed many of the recurring themes we have seen in our workshops.

Please don't take this book too seriously. And, please don't believe what we say. Lord knows none of us needs another belief system. If you like, you can pretend you are reading a fantasy fiction novel, a mystery or perhaps a good Sci-Fi.

And maybe, just maybe, you will bump into yourself along the way.

Ariel & Shya Kane

"HOW CAN I BE SURE?

IN A WORLD THAT'S

CONSTANTLY CHANGING,

HOW CAN I BE SURE?..."

THE YOUNG RASCALS

HOW CAN I BE SURE?

THE CHOICES WE FACE TODAY ARE CERTAINLY MORE baffling than they were years ago when societal roles were fairly pre-set, and people could blindly follow the cultural prescription. Increasingly, individuals have the power to make their own way. As we each travel down our own unique path, questions arise: Is what I am doing right? Am I with the right person? Is this the job for me? Do I want children? Should I move? How can I be sure...

With the vast array of possibilities facing us today, we want to feel confident that our choices are good ones. We want to be strong in ourselves but not rigid. We want to feel as if our lives have direction, purpose and meaning. We read, search and exchange ideas in hopes of being centered, being productive and feeling vital. We are looking for that which would transform a mundane existence into an exciting, breathtaking adventure, searching for peace of mind, health and satisfaction. What people are pining for in their secret hearts has been described by sages throughout the ages as Enlightenment and Self-Realization. There are other synonyms, too. Try nirvana, waking up, the Great Way, heaven on earth, Christ Consciousness or realizing your Higher Self.

The two of us have spent the better part of our adult lives in search of the miraculous. We hungered for that state of being wherein satisfaction, self-expression and creativity reside. We took countless workshops and traveled to be with masters all over the world in search of this elusive state, only to discover that Enlightenment, Self-Realization and Self-Satisfaction are coexistent with our present state of being.

HEAVEN ON EARTH IS HAPPENING
SIMULTANEOUSLY WITH THE WAY OUR LIVES ARE
SHOWING UP, RIGHT NOW IN THIS MOMENT.
THE TRICK IS TO BE ABLE TO
ACCESS THIS COEXISTING STATE, DAY IN, DAY OUT,
MOMENT-BY-MOMENT, NOT JUST WHEN IN
PLEASANT, IDEAL CIRCUMSTANCES

GETTING TO THE MOMENT

IN THE FOLLOWING PAGES, WE WILL DEFINE THE KEYS WHICH OPEN the door to living in the moment that will facilitate a transformational shift, enabling you to live a more effective, productive and satisfying life. We will also outline impediments to living in a vital and alive manner.

PARADOX AND CONFUSION

It has been said that the doors to enlightenment are guarded by two lions. One of the lions represents paradox. As you read on, you may find some ideas seem paradoxical -- in other words it may seem that we are presenting two ideas that are directly in opposition to one another. A paradox is where these two seem-ingly contradictory ideas can both be true. For example take the saying, "water, water everywhere and not a drop to drink." One might think if there is water everywhere, of course you could drink it. Yet, if you were floating in the middle of the ocean on a leaky raft, this statement would not only be true but also make perfect sense. The other lion represents confusion. It is likely that you will find some of the concepts in this book confusing at first. This is a natural process because anything that is new does not always make immediate sense since it is outside of what is already known. We apologize for any confusion in advance.

LISTENING YOUR WAY TO THE MOMENT

One way to access the moment is to truly hear what others are saying. If you listen newly to each individual conversation, the act of listening can shift your life, instantaneously.

In the case of this book, listening becomes reading. Perhaps what we are talking about here is not new, but then again, perhaps it is.

TRUE LISTENING IS ACTIVELY LISTENING
TO ANOTHER WITH THE INTENTION
OF HEARING WHAT IS BEING SAID
FROM THE <u>SPEAKER'S</u> POINT OF VIEW

When reading this, if you could view the information as fresh, and actually hear what we are saying, your whole life could transform in an instant.

In Zen, there is a term "beginner's mind". In the beginner's mind there is not the preconception of already knowing or having heard something before. There is only the possibility of something new, of something heretofore unseen.

COMPARISON

Comparison limits the possibility of living in the moment. The mind compares this moment to its memory bank of moments. When it is grappling with something new or unfamiliar, the mind finds something it knows which it perceives as a reasonable facsimile and then groups the two together. This is always off target.

At best, it cuts out the nuances of living, and it is in the nuances that the richness of life is born. At worst, our interpretations are totally inaccurate.

24

When a friend of ours was little, she heard the song, "My bonnie lies over the ocean." She had never heard of a "bonnie". It wasn't in her vocabulary. So, instead, she interpreted what she heard as, "My *body* lies over the ocean. My *body* lies over the sea." Hearing the words she thought were part of the song would always bring to her mind images of someone floating on his or her back in the calm blue ocean. Now, as an adult, she realizes that she misinterpreted the lyrics. What seemed similar or the same, was not the same at all. Whether we are old or young, our minds still function like that.

WHERE ARE YOU?

Let's say you don't know where you are in New York City and you want to get to 72nd Street and Broadway. You can have a road map and you can find out where Broadway and 72nd cross but that alone won't help you. First, you have to know where you are. If you don't know where you are in this moment, you'll never find where you want to get to.

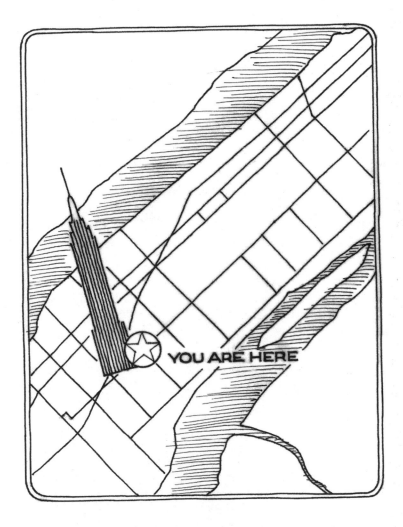

The starting point is to discover where you are. And then, when you know where you are in this moment, something can shift. This takes a degree of surrender to how the circumstances in your life are showing up.

When you are in water, if you relax, it floats you. If you struggle, if you tense up, you sink and drown. Well, it's that way with life.

If you are present with what's happening in your life in each moment, life supports you totally. But if you are worrying about possible futures, you're not present. It's as if you're breathing in when you're underwater. You sink and drown. That's why many people's lives feel overwhelming to them. It is a function of trying to live their lives right rather than noticing who they're with, what they're doing or where they are in their lives in this moment.

NOTICING OR NEUTRALLY

OBSERVING YOUR LIFE

WITHOUT TRYING TO MANIPULATE

OR CHANGE WHAT YOU SEE

IS ACTUALLY THE ESSENCE OR

KEY COMPONENT OF TRANSFORMATION.

ANOTHER WORD FOR THIS

NON - JUDGMENTAL SEEING

IS AWARENESS.

AWARENESS

People don't need to work on themselves. They just have to notice, to be aware. What it takes to wake up or transform is to bring awareness to whatever is going on in your life in the moment. "Bringing awareness" does not mean you have to do something with what you become aware of. You don't have to do anything about it. You don't have to fix it or change it.

This is a hard concept for people to understand because often when people see something about themselves they perceive as negative, they judge it and don't like it and try to change it. This is not awareness. Awareness is neutral.

When you become aware of a mechanical behavior such

as biting your nails and just notice it, the automaticity actually fades away and then you are left with you, acting appropriately, choosing whether or not to continue that behavior.

THE PHENOMENON OF TRANSFORMATION

Transformation doesn't actually happen through words. Transformation is an experience, not a concept. But the mind can only hold concepts. For example, the difference between *actually* being on a warm sunny beach and *thinking* about being on a warm sunny beach is profound.

Experiences naturally devolve into concepts. In order to maintain something other than a temporary shift, there has to be a letting go of the habitual ways of thinking. Otherwise, the mind catches up with any transformation, compensates for it, and you are back where you started. That is why people have had peak experiences -- and they've been just that -- a peak that doesn't last. They are out of their mechanical way of relating for a bit, but then the mind gets back in control and they go right back into the old systems of behavior and everything is the same as it ever was.

There was a fellow who once came to an Instantaneous Transformation® seminar which we presented. From his perspective, the evening had a magical quality. He was suddenly less worried. At work the following week, he got things done with little or no effort. He was sleeping well for the first time in years. He felt in sync with his whole life.

A year later, he came to another seminar very angry at us. "It was supposed to be instantaneous," he said. "It only lasted for a couple of weeks."

This man was looking for a magic pill. He wanted to swallow it once and then not have to pay attention to how he was living for the rest of his life. What engendered the shift in the first place was that our seminar was an environment where this fellow was able to look at himself without finding fault with what he saw. The seminar acted as a neutral light, illuminating what simply was in his life so that he could see it without judgment.

The awareness that was brought forth in this group produced an instantaneous shift. But awareness is not a one time thing. Bringing awareness to how you are relating to yourself and your environment is a way of life. If you want transformational shifts to last, you must support them. You wouldn't expect to go to the gym and say "Wow, what a great workout. Well that should take care of exercise for the next 5 or 10 years. See ya next decade." The ability to live moment-to-moment is like an underused skill-set or muscle. With practice it becomes strong and you are able to have stamina and endurance.

31

This is paradoxical. On the one hand, working on yourself doesn't work. On the other hand, you must be engaged in your life and aware of how you are living in order to have transformation be a lasting and expanding experience.

CHANGE - VS - TRANSFORMATION

In the past, transformation was an obscure word, but this term has really made it into the mainstream in the last few years. It's gotten so that people think change and transformation are pretty much the same - but they're not.

We, as authors, are not trying to get you to manipulate your language so you say the *right* words after reading this book. Rather, we feel it is important that you know what we are talking about when using the term "transformation" as opposed to "change". This next section is devoted to delineating the differences between the two so that you will be able to recognize and support the state of transformation.

Transformation can only be instantaneous. Anything that happens over time is change. Change is incremental and linear. It takes place in time. Transformation, on the other hand, is an immediate exponential shift, like a shifting of states and it goes forward and backward in time. It is a shift, like a molecule of water which goes from liquid to solid at the instant it hits 32 degrees Fahrenheit.

Change is an incremental, linear progression. It happens over time. It is directed. It is measurable. It is provable. It is logical. It happens sequentially. Change follows the laws of cause and effect.

Transformation, on the other hand, is exponential, not incremental. It happens everywhere at once. It is not linear. It happens outside of time. It is instantaneous.

Change is past/future oriented whereas transformation is

now. Transformation is only now and it can only happen now, in the present moment. You cannot work on yourself to transform. Change involves *doing* something, and transformation is a way of *being*.

WHEN YOU GET HERE
-- TO THIS MOMENT OF NOW --
EACH DAY BECOMES EXTRAORDINARY
IT IS PROFOUND AND ORDINARY
AT THE SAME TIME

Being in the moment allows you to *include* the conflicts that arise in your day, the body sensations, emotions, etc. For instance, there are days when you do not feel well, but when you are living your life moment-to-moment, you can include uncomfortable feelings and sensations and still experience well-being.

A lot of people have the erroneous idea that when you transform you are never ill and you don't die -- you ascend. They think you should never get angry or be upset. This is not the case. When you really discover how to get here, you can integrate anything that is happening in your life, so there is a state of well-being which you experience and out of which you live.

What allows you to transform is awareness.

AWARENESS IS A NON-JUDGMENTAL
WITNESSING, VIEWING OR SEEING OF YOURSELF
AND HOW YOU INTERACT WITH YOUR LIFE

The Instantaneous Transformation® technology is based on awareness. While change is psychological in nature and problem/solution oriented, transformation is anthropological. The job of anthropologists is to simply notate what they see in a culture or a tribe without judgmental interpretation. For example, they might say, "The tribe ate roasted grubs this morning at 6AM." This is a simple observation. A good anthropologist wouldn't say, "First thing these heathens did today was eat those disgusting grubs."

What we are suggesting is that there is an "isness" to things that is not culturally determined. Through awareness, you can notice what *is*, not what you consider beautiful or ugly, appealing or disgusting. What keeps you from discovering the isness of things is your judgments and prejudices.

CHANGE	-VS-	TRANSFORMATION
Happens Over Time		Instantaneous
Past/Future		Present Moment
Linear/Incremental		Exponential/Quantum
Psychological Cause/Effect		Anthropological Observation/Awareness
Judgmental		Non-judgmental
Dichotomous Good/Bad Right/Wrong Positive/Negative Win/Lose		Based in what Is/Isness
Mind/Survival Based		Self/Aliveness Based
Reasonable/Logical		Unreasonable/Intuitive
Goal/Doing Oriented		Being Oriented
Problem/Solution		Isness
Decisions		Choices
Manipulative		Creative
Reactive		Proactive
Exclusive		Inclusive
Hierarchical		Partnership/Team

35

PREJUDICES

If you want to become aware of your mechanical behaviors, a

good place to start is to look honestly at your prejudices. False beliefs, ignorance and prejudices keep individuals locked in repeating patterns. Sometimes it is even the prejudice against prejudice that keeps people stuck. Have you ever heard someone emphatically state, "I am not prejudiced!"? Inherent in that statement is the subtext, "Only 'bad' people or 'stupid' people are prejudiced and surely I am not one of those." If you judge your prejudices as wrong, you will be putting on blinders. You won't readily see the truth about how you mechanically operate in your life because you won't want to be wrong. This path leads to ignorance.

THE DICTIONARY
DEFINES ENLIGHTENMENT AS:
TO FREE OF IGNORANCE, FALSE BELIEF
OR PREJUDICE

To deny that each and every one of us has prejudices is akin to pretending that we don't breathe. How about the statement, "Wow, what a beautiful figure!" In Bali, many women dream of having a curvaceous bottom and prominent hips while in the United States, women are working diligently to trim those hips and that derrière. Have you ever considered that your picture of the ideal woman or ideal man might be a culturally based prejudice that could inhibit your ability to relate? Perhaps it hasn't occurred to most that thinking someone has "beautiful" eyes can be a prejudice too.

A prejudice, according to the dictionary, is simply "an opinion formed beforehand or without knowledge or thought." If you want to discover your own doorway to enlightenment, you have to be willing to see your cultural and familial beliefs and prejudices and then have the courage to find what is actually true for you.

TAKING OFF THE BLINDERS

Part of the process of freeing yourself from blindly following your inculturated way of viewing life is to discover what you are resisting. For example, if you choose a path in opposition to someone, such as a parent, or in opposition to a group, such as a church, you narrow the way you can behave in your life to one option. This

option is to be "not like them". Rather than having infinite possibilities and life choices available, your behavior becomes con-
stricted to the polar opposite of that which you are resisting.
Ever heard of the terms "dead set against" and "dead right"? It is
not surprising that both of these phrases use the word dead.
When one is set in a position that allows for no other possibility,
it kills off aliveness and spirit, wonder and creativity.

38

BEING RIGHT - VS - BEING ALIVE

As an analogy, you could say that there are two houses in which
to live but you can only dwell in one of them. There is the Right
house and there is the Alive house.

In the Right house, you get to be "right", righteously
right. Not necessarily correct, but always right. In other words,
your point of view is the only possible one and anybody who
doesn't agree with your perspective is "wrong".

In the Alive house, you get to experience love, health,
happiness, full self-expression, satisfaction, relationship, etc.

To live in either of these houses, you must pay rent. In order to live in the Right house, the rent you have to pay is: giving up the experience of love, health, happiness, full self-expression, satisfaction, relationship, etc.

39

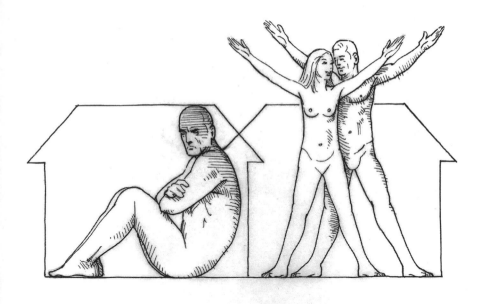

In order to live in the Alive house, you have to give up being "right". That is all it takes to have an alive, joyous life. You must simply be willing to let go of the need to have the point of view that you are right dominate all aspects of your life. This is especially challenging when you are, in fact, correct. But if you have to prove another is wrong, even if you win, you lose. Something inside you is less alive.

THE DEATH OF THE PAST

MOST OF US HAVE A STRONG ATTACHMENT TO OUR
story of what happened in the past, and often don't recognize
how powerfully this story affects our lives. We are not only
attached to memories of the good times, but also to memories of
the bad times. There is a fear that if we let go of it all, we will be
less interesting or that we won't know who we are anymore --
that something important about us will die. In order to move
into our full potential as human beings, there has to be a letting
go of what we already know. Most people hold on to what they
know for fear they won't survive. What keeps us stuck in the
same old stories is that we never let them complete themselves.
Waking up, the ability to live in the moment, is a dying of the
old, the old way in which we perceive our lives. There has to be

a stepping out of our attachment to the past in order to discover who we are in this moment.

MEMORIES: FACT OR FICTION

Let us investigate memories for a moment. A common misconception is that our memories are an accurate representation of past events. But in fact, they are simply recordings of those events made from the point of view of the person we were at that time.

Hasn't your life expanded in the past 5 or 10 years? If the answer to this question is yes, then even your truest memories were set in place by a more limited version of yourself, and like a tape which has been repeatedly played, have distorted over time. Certainly, childhood memories of disagreements or injustices we experienced were, at best, originally told in that child's voice from a young and immature perspective. Each retelling of this story, to ourselves in our thoughts or out loud to others, has been modified by the point of view we possessed at the time of retelling.

Here is another example of how our memories can actually be distortions, as told from Shya's point of view:

43

Once I built a house in Maine. It was way back in the woods and you needed to have a four-wheel-drive vehicle to get to it. I built my home on the foundation of an old farmhouse that had existed there many years before.

One day an old man came down the road and said, "I used to live here many years ago when I was just a boy. I would really like it if I could look around. May I?"

I said, "Sure." He was excited.

"There was a great big cellar hole that was maybe 50 feet by 50 feet -- it was huge," he told me.

So we went to take a look at the cellar over which I had built my house. The real dimensions were about 20 feet by 20 feet. The old man was shocked.

"This couldn't be! This is so small. Where I grew up was much bigger. It was huge!"

As we climbed the cellar stairs into the light, the man was shaking his head in disbelief.

"There was a well," he said next. "It was at least 40 or 50 feet deep."

There was only one well on our property. I had a hard time cleaning it out when I first arrived. I had to dig out mud, old leaves and debris to clean it down to the bedrock. I took him to the well. Actually, the depth was only eight or nine feet.

45

⌒   ⌒   ⌒

To a child, eight or nine feet can look like 50 feet. But it is just a distortion from a child's point of view.

IF YOU BELIEVE YOUR VERSION OF THE PAST
YOU WILL BE LIVING YOUR LIFE BUILT ON LIES

Recent studies have conclusively shown that "false" memories can be remembered even more clearly than actual ones.

At Western Washington University, scientists conducted an experiment where researchers told test subjects that they would be asked a series of questions about events from their childhood and the answers would be compared with their family members' memories of the same events.

Here is the catch. Unbeknownst to the test subjects, the investigators asked about an event that had, in fact, never happened. The researchers asked about a time when the participant had, as a child, been to a wedding reception and spilled the punch bowl on the mother of the bride. Initially, none of the participants had a recollection of this incident.

Later, the same subjects were re-interviewed. Surprisingly, this fictitious event could now be recalled. At this time, some of the participants even "remembered" specific details about the bogus episode.

Researchers have also found that false memories can be created by combining an actual memory with a suggestion made by someone.

Reading about these studies explained certain experiences the two of us have had with our own clients. For example, one of our clients, Tom, the president of a family owned business, told us that as a child he had a demanding father who regularly humiliated him. He cited, as an example, the time the father mowed the lawn because he felt that Tom had not been thorough enough in his initial cutting. When we discussed this incident further, Tom realized that his father, who was a heart surgeon, was a very precise man. Tom saw that his dad had not intended to embarrass him but indeed had wanted the yard to meet his standards of perfection. With his adult eyes, Tom realized that his father's standards were not unreasonable but that actually he, as a ten year old, not really wanting to mow the lawn in the first place, had done a less than satisfactory job. Subsequently, Tom, who had been estranged from his father, made overtures to reconcile their relationship. In doing so, he discovered that his father was much nicer and more tolerant than he remembered him to be. In fact, he is a great man and Tom shares many of his traits.

Now, enter Tom's brother, Jim. Jim worked for the family enterprise in a different country. We were called in for a consultation when the brothers met at the corporate headquarters. During the conversation, we were surprised to hear Jim relate the same story about the mowing of the lawn and his demanding, humiliating father as if it had happened to him. It was told with the same intensity, sentence structure and cadence as Tom's version. It was so amazingly similar that we questioned both of them about their stories. What we uncovered was that neither brother had an exact recollection of the event. In fact, the story had been related to them by their eldest sister who had "seen it all." Until that moment, it never occurred to either man that their whole attitude about their father had been shaped to fit the point of view of their sister. They had "remembered" what had been told to them over time as if it was their own experience.

There is a classic film, *Rashomon*, directed by Akira Kurosawa, which explores similar themes. This Japanese movie, from the early 50's, depicts an incident that takes place between a man, his wife, and a brigand, played by Toshiro Mifune. Each of these three characters lives through the same event together. Yet each person's story supports his or her point of view and memory of what happened. Eventually, the viewer finds out what actually transpired and it is vastly different from each participant's version. Our memories are biased by our agendas and points of view and if we hold our memories as the "Truth" we will surely be misguided.

INSTANTANEOUS
TRANSFORMATION®

BY NOW, YOU MAY BE ASKING, "OKAY, HOW DOES Instantaneous Transformation® really work?"

The following is a story, told from Ariel's point of view, which illustrates Instantaneous Transformation® in action. It takes place on the island of Bali in Indonesia where the two of us were speakers at a conference. Jody was an attendee at the event. She scheduled a private consulting session with us and when she showed up at our room, none of us expected what would come next.

It was about four o'clock and the sun shone through the

window of our room at the Nusa Dua Beach Hotel. I was glad that we had air conditioning because I wasn't used to the heat nor the humidity. Although we were in Bali, Indonesia for the Second Annual Earth Conference, 12,000 miles away from home, as Jody came into the room, all of that fell away. Hotel rooms have a way of doing that. Some are much nicer than others but all in all, they have an anonymity and an ability to drop out of time. The background, the town, and even the country can all recede, leaving just you. It is almost as if those rooms are empty vessels waiting to be filled with thousands of moments from thousands of lives. I rarely think of them as a sanctuary, or a place for a profound healing to take place, but they can be that, too.

Jody, a slim woman with curly dark hair streaked with lively gray highlights, was a little nervous when she came in.

"Why did you book a session with us, Jody? What did you want to have happen for you here?" Shya asked once we all were seated.

"I don't know. People have recommended I give it a try, that I will really like it. I have heard that you do different types of sessions. That you speak with people about issues or consult businesses. But I also heard that you do some amazing pain relief and frankly I am very sore from hauling my luggage around. My bags are really heavy. I don't know what to expect but I was sort of hoping you could get rid of the pain in my shoulders."

"OK, Jody, let's get out the massage table. You can lie face down and let's see what we can do for you."

I knew that what we were about to do would seem like a type of massage, but actually this pain relief technique, which Shya created, is a form of modern day alchemy. In ancient alchemy, the philosopher's stone was something that was supposed to transmute lead or base metals into gold. Our technique is like the philosopher's stone. As Jody allowed herself to be with the pain and tension in her body, it disappeared -- instantaneously.

We chatted and worked the tension out of her muscles, never really going anywhere, just letting her get in touch with what was there. As Jody felt each spot that we found, it melted away.

About a half an hour into the session, Shya pressed on a tight spot in Jody's neck. I had a hand on her lower back and was

just basically hanging out at that point. She seemed to be holding her breath.

"Take a deep breath, through your mouth and up into your
chest," I said quietly near her ear and I felt a wave of sadness.
"What is it, Jody -- are you seeing something in your mind's
eye?"

Jody took a ragged breath. Almost mouthing the words,
they were so faint, she said, "It's so stupid. It's so stupid."

I didn't know what she was talking about, but that did-
n't matter. "It's OK that it's stupid, let yourself feel this spot."

"It's OK to be sad," Shya finished.

Like a baby who draws in a massive amount of breath,
just before letting out a tremendous wail, Jody pulled in a lung
full of air and silently began to sob.

"It's OK, honey, you can make noise if you want to," I murmured
into her ear.

I wouldn't be surprised if someone passing by our door heard a young child bawling its eyes out because that was how it sounded to me. Sobs racked her body and we were just there with her. It's funny how good it felt to be with Jody then. It was almost a holy feeling as if the source of life itself had been touched somehow. Her weeping was the sound of a forgotten soul coming home after having been left outside in the cold for a long, long time.

53

"What's happening in the picture you are seeing, Jody?" Shya gently prompted again.

"I touched Daddy's cigarettes." The last word melted into another set of sobs which lasted for some time. Eventually, the crying ebbed and Jody began to regain her control.

"It's so stupid!" she said again.

"It doesn't matter if the picture seems stupid to your adult mind, Jody. Don't judge it. For whatever reason, it was important to a younger version of you."

"I touched Daddy's cigarettes."

"OK, how old were you?"

"Maybe 18 months. Something like that."

"OK, then what happened?"

"Well, Daddy slapped my hand. And -- and then he died."

This would explain the tears. Shya and I looked at each other. We knew then that it was likely there was more to this emotional puzzle which Jody hadn't seen yet.

"When did he die? What happened?"

"Well, he slapped my hand and then he had a heart attack about an hour later."

"And what did you think that meant?"

"I... I killed him."

As the sobs began anew, they held less intensity this time. Quietly, we waited for the storm to subside. Eventually, the downpour softened and then petered out. There was a clean quality in the air as if something had been cleansed, much like a soaking rain will drench the earth and wash away the dust, leaving things sparkling in its wake.

55

"Now run the picture again through your mind like a movie, only this time, watch it with your adult eyes. Tell us what you see."

As Jody recounted the tale it had lost most of its emotional intensity.

"My Daddy smoked. I can see the package. They were Lucky Strikes. It was in the living room. I reached for them and then," she took a deep breath "then, Daddy slapped my hand. I knew I had done something terribly naughty. He died right after that and I thought that my naughtiness did it. I killed him."

"Jody, did you really kill your father? Did you have anything to do with it at all?"

Jody paused for a moment and sighed, "No, no I didn't. I just thought I did."

A little while later, when Jody sat up, she looked years younger. She perched rather shakily on the edge of the massage table so we told her to take her time. We didn't want her to rush and get things back together. That memory had been buried, waiting to surface for a long, long time. Jody looked as new as the baby she had been all those years ago.

"You guys, that's amazing! I never thought of that before. Ever! How did you do that?"

Shya looked at me and I at him. With a slight smile we shrugged.

"Actually Jody, we didn't *do* anything. We just hung out with you and with whatever was happening in your neck. We just sort of tricked you into the moment and whatever was left over in your body from your childhood surfaced to be looked at and experienced. Sometimes memories seem to be stored in a person's body. By touching a place of tension and allowing you to feel what is there, it can dissolve. In your case, it seems this memory was triggered by the spot in your neck but we weren't looking for it nor were we trying to get rid of it once you touched upon it."

I sat next to her and took her hand. "How do you feel?"

Jody's gaze turned inward for a moment. "New. I feel new."

We all sat there for a bit, not saying anything, just savoring the silence, the newness and the richness of simply being alive.

"I have always felt sad. I never knew why before."

"Ahh, Jody." Shya said with a gentle smile, "Don't blame your sadness on what you saw here today. You were just sad, that's all. How are you -- do you feel sad now?"

"No. I don't. I feel..." She began searching for the right word to describe her state. Things had slowed down for the three of us. "I feel grateful," she said with a smile, "and I feel curiously empty."

We both nodded. We knew this state well. It is as if some secret place deep inside has been holding onto a piece of the past and when this old relic is finally cleared out, it makes space in your heart to experience life anew.

As she stood up, her whole body had rearranged itself. Before it was as if she had been protecting a deep hurt. No amount of massage could affect the kind of transformation that had happened when she simply let go of her judgment that what she saw and felt was "stupid" and let herself feel what was there in her heart.

Jody fairly toddled her way out into the late afternoon Balinese sun. She looked like she was finding a whole new set of legs on which to stand and as I saw her making her way quietly down to the ocean, I felt privileged -- privileged to be alive and blessed that Jody had let us be a part of her own rebirth.

A NEW REALITY

Part of what was so beautiful about the experience with Jody was that it was unplanned and was not a part of some agenda of hers or ours. We didn't think that there was anything wrong with her that needed to be fixed.

All we did was be present with her in a way that allowed her to observe herself in a non-judgmental way. We acted as catalytic agents that allowed her to get into the moment. And when Jody got into the moment, without judging what she saw, her life transformed.

A therapist who was attending one of our seminars once told us that it was clear that we had regressed Jody back to her childhood and obviously it had some therapeutic results. Actually, we didn't "do" anything. None of us were expecting to visit Jody's childhood. It just showed up in the moment.

BEING IN THE MOMENT

The agreement in this society is that your past has molded you to the way you are now. One of the major components that keeps people from experiencing this moment is the attachment to their life story which generally blames someone or something for how they are today. The common misconception is that there has got to be a good reason for why you are the way you are. But what if there is no reason?

Sometimes people repeat a story for years, "I am an angry person because my mother hit me when I was four," and the retelling of the story does nothing to lessen the anger. If you allow yourself simply to *feel* what it is to be angry without judging it or blaming it on the past or past circumstances, then the anger will fade and will lose its hold over you.

After her session with us, Jody wrote and published an article detailing her experience and the resulting transformation. Once it appeared in a magazine, we had a wave of people who came to us with the agenda to fix their "screwed up" childhoods. The majority of these people came proving that their parents raised them wrong. It was challenging for them because the agenda to be *right* that their parents were *wrong* was often actually stronger than the desire to dissolve the "problem".

You can't fix your childhood. It's over -- finished. All of those stories you have from growing up, even the good ones, are all a distortion of a child's mind anyway. Remember the man who came to look at the cellar hole and the well at Shya's farm in Maine? Well, the visit to his childhood home "dis-illusioned" that man. In other words, the illusions, which he had held as truths from a child's memory, were dispelled.

LOOKING AT YOUR LIFE THROUGH A

TRANSFORMATIONAL FRAMEWORK

IS PARADOXICAL

FOR EXAMPLE: TRAUMATIC INCIDENTS

IN YOUR PAST HAVE AFFECTED YOUR LIFE. HOWEVER,

YOU CAN'T BLAME HOW YOU ARE BEING

IN THIS MOMENT ON YOUR PAST

FORGIVENESS

Now let's look at a fundamental element for transforming your life: Forgiving your parents for anything they did wrong or you think they did wrong. Actually, forgiving the past. Since the memories of your childhood are distortions held over time, the past and your childhood and how your parents or siblings related to you become irrelevant.

This is a radical departure from working on your history to bring about change. This is where we jump from a psychological framework to an anthropological one. (An anthropologist notates, or neutrally observes what he or she sees without trying to change what is seen.)

This is also where our attachments to our stories become evident. Someone might say, "But I know I am a good reader because my mother read to me everyday." But is that *true* or is this individual just a good reader because they are? On the other end of the spectrum, an individual might feel that they are a failure in relationship because they were a victim of child abuse or the product of a broken home.

Over the years, the two of us have seen folks from all walks of life, including those who have survived sexual abuse, physical abuse and even concentration camps, discover how to have the traumas of their past no longer hold sway over their lives and life choices made today.

FORGIVENESS:
1. TO GIVE UP RESENTMENT AGAINST OR THE DESIRE TO
PUNISH; STOP BEING ANGRY WITH; PARDON
2. TO CANCEL A DEBT - TO MAKE AS IF
THE DEBT NEVER HAPPENED

Part of the reason most children so severely judge their parents is that it is impossible, by virtue of age and lack of maturity, to share an adult perspective. Later, when grown, earlier judgments and ways of being are firmly entrenched and rarely investigated.

Things that seem odd or inappropriate, when viewed from the outside, would make sense if you had the capacity to step inside the psyche, logic system and life circumstances of your parent (or any other person).

If you could *be* them rather than judging them from the outside or looking at them through the idea that you know who they are, you might discover a place of compassion for how difficult it is to be a human being on planet earth.

Ideally, we should feel warm towards and close to all of those we care about. But sometimes hurtful things have been done or said that have created a distance and we have grown apart. It is hard to understand when people we love disappoint or hurt us. Sometimes their actions seem so unreasonable and inexplicable that we find it nearly impossible to let them back into our hearts. And yet, most of us feel a longing for closeness.

One of the best gifts you can give to yourself and to others is the gift of forgiveness. If you could actually walk a mile in another's shoes, you could find a place of understanding that would allow you to regain what has been lost.

In 1993, Shya's mother, Ida, passed away. The time prior to and around her death was surprisingly rich and rewarding. It was a time for many discoveries and forgivenesses. It was a passage where secrets were told and puzzles unraveled. We would like to share this precious experience with you as told from Ariel's point of view.

IDA

IDA WAS NO LONGER BREATHING. THE ARTERY IN HER NECK STILL pulsed steadily and I leaned in, calmly watching her lips tinge blue. I knew it would only be a few more moments. Shya's mother, Ida, had been in and out of the hospital for some time. At age 84 her own doctor had likened her heart to a tire which was old and worn; it was ready to blow at any time. Max, Shya's father, had understandably been very upset by that analogy. Although this comparison might have been insensitive, I felt the doctor was trying his best to prepare Max for the inevitable.

For more than 50 years Max and Ida had been working together. As a young bookkeeper, Ida had spotted Max who was then a young cutter in the garment district. A cutter lays out the patterns over layers of material and then cuts the shapes to be sewn. On the day Max asked her for a date, I am told that she agreed to go out with him provided he would bring her a pattern for one of the hot new spring dresses. Max fulfilled the request and it was the beginning of a long and fruitful relationship.

I sometimes wonder what Ida did with that pattern. Sewing wasn't one of her strong suits. By the time I met her, she had taken to embellishing sweaters by appliquéing diamond shaped swatches of material in contrasting color to the front, bordering the patches with bric-a-brac of yet another color and then she would finish the job by sewing in a designer label, purloined from Max's dress factory. Ida had an amazing array of hats, sweaters and the like which I am sure Bill Blass, Scaasi, Vera Wang and Carolina Herrara would have cringed to see his or her designer label upon.

Her decline had taken a number of years. At first, it was not so obvious. When she was 80, Ida still worked two days a week as the bookkeeper at the Max Kane Dress Company in New York City's garment district where her husband made designer dresses, wedding and ball gowns.

The shifts in Ida's health and mental state are frozen in slide-like time segments of factory life. Shya and I frequently visited them there. Although from time to time they came and visited us at our home, we most often saw them at what Ida and Max had come to call "the place".

On one such visit, Ida thoroughly surprised us by asking, "What do you need? If you need money for anything, just let me know and I'll help you. Just don't tell Mr. Kane." She always called Max "Mr. Kane" at the factory, even to us.

The offer for money was quite a shock to Shya. Never in his young or adult life had there been such an offer. When he was growing up, money had been very tight and the first clothes he ever owned that were not bought second-hand were from money he earned himself at age 15. Spartan spending when buying clothes was only the tip of the iceberg when it came to Ida's way with money, but I will get to that later.

So, we took Ida up on her offer. We were very grateful for the assistance, but we honored her request not to tell Mr. Kane.

Eventually, during some of our weekly visits to the place, Ida would, as usual, chat about how business was and talk about the different orders they had in-house. Quite suddenly she would start talking about a designer that Max hadn't worked for in ten or fifteen years, thinking the orders were current news. It was as if the needle on an old record player had mysteriously skipped grooves and was back playing a previous song. Time was no longer progressing linearly for Ida. We began to be concerned about her ability to keep the books as it seemed to be more and more stressing for her. Around about this time, she and Shya had a very frank conversation.

The rows of sewing machines hummed and vibrated in the background as we sat in her little office under the fluorescent light. "Mom, I am concerned about something," he began. "What if you become sick or incapacitated? Who will know about your and Dad's finances? Does he know what stocks you have or where the accounts are held?"

Of course the answer was no. Ida had been very secretive over the years. It was obvious there were stocks because dividend checks came to the house. All of the envelopes she then kept rubber-banded together in piles because, she said, "You never know when you might need scrap paper." Since we were at the factory, Ida took a big sheet of pattern paper upon which she drew some grids and as we sat with her, she made a list of assets. It was obvious that much was missing, but it was a start.

Eventually Ida started staying home. It was too much of a trip to travel into the city and she had begun falling. Luckily, Max was still strong enough to lift her. All the years of working and cutting had kept the 5'3" man robust. But he began to worry for her safety when he was gone, so he hired daytime help to keep her company and keep her safe.

Ida's physical decline which had led inexorably to this hospital bed had been at times graceful and others difficult or painful. For instance, it was painful for a formerly self-sufficient person to stop driving. No one wanted to tell her to stop, to take away that freedom. Finally, she mistook reverse for park and, thinking she had parked the car, she got out. The car reversed, the door knocked her over as it rolled backward, and it was time. She never drove again.

She hated giving up the bookkeeping, too, but she was no longer able to make the computations. At Ida's insistence,

Max brought the work home for her at first, but soon she would get agitated and fret over it so he stopped and got a bookkeeper in the city. Before long, it was time for another honest conversation. Oh, these talks could be difficult! How does one bring up with a parent, or anyone for that matter, their mortality, their failing health and diminishing mental capabilities. This is not something most of us are trained to do. I am sure my parents felt similarly when they had to broach subjects that were embarrassing or agitating to me as I was growing up. Yes, the roles were finally and irrevocably reversing. We were now operating as parents, acting in what we hoped was Ida's best interest as she was rapidly assuming the role of child.

"Mom, we need to sort out your finances," Shya bravely began on one telephone call. "Where do you keep your stock certificates and records?"

She fidgeted and hemmed and hawed but eventually it was determined they were kept at home, in the freezer. This brought to mind funny images such as certificates frozen in blocks of ice and phrases like "cool cash" and "frozen assets". We knew we were out of our depth. It would take someone more knowledgeable to help sort things out. So we enlisted the aid of our accountant and friend, Josh Blau, to come out with us and raid the fridge.

A week or two later found us at Ida's house. I wasn't fond of sitting on the plastic slip covers Ida used to protect the living room furniture, so I had her join me in the dining nook where we chatted as Shya and Josh checked the freezer. That was when we discovered the freezer was bare. Had she hidden things? Was this a new game, perhaps of hide and seek? But no, Ida appeared guileless. Maybe she only remembered it as in the freezer. It was time to hunt.

When I was young, my sisters and I would sometimes hide something and one or the other of us would look for the concealed object. Then the person who had camouflaged the item would give feedback as we searched, "You are getting warmer, warmer, hotter," etc. if we moved toward the hiding place or "You are getting cold, colder, ice cold," as we moved away.

Well, the freezer was pretty warm, but not the actual stashing spot. Next to the freezer was an old brown shopping bag. This bag was hot, red hot. In this bag was years and years of accumulated financial information.

Sorting through this brown paper safety deposit box turned out to be a dangerous mission. Ida had, unwittingly, booby-trapped the bag to would-be intruders. See, Ida didn't see the need to buy paper clips. Being at a clothing factory she had an endless supply of fine, sharp straight pins. Many times Josh did not need to pluck out a record. As he withdrew his hand from this grown-up version of a grab bag, the record would automatically come along, its pin embedded in a finger or thumb.

Old crumbling bits of doilies, linoleum, fabrics and old, old stocks like Studebaker still lived in that bag. There were other bags there, too. Suddenly things began to come clear. Envelopes and rubber bands were not the only things that Ida had collected. There in those bags, unbeknownst to her children or even Mr. Kane, Ida had amassed a small fortune. Well, that is not quite true. To be honest, the fortune was more than a small one. Max was shocked.

"She still gets upset when I buy Minute Maid Orange Juice instead of a cheaper store brand," was his comment that I remember most.

So a piece of the puzzle had fallen into place and a picture was starting to emerge. Now I knew why she never wanted us to tell Mr. Kane about those previous gifts. She hadn't wanted him to suspect she had money to spend.

Months later, in the hospital that day as I sat there, waiting at her bedside, watching her lips grow blue, I knew we were at a passage.

The moment was coming, again, and holding Ida's hand I leaned directly into her line of sight so that my face was positioned close in front of hers. It was important that she knew she was not alone. Here it came, the gasp, the reflexive gripping of my hand as Ida returned from her journey, sucking in a panicked breath as the body, which was not quite ready to relinquish its hold over her, reasserted its need for oxygen.

I had been with Ida for several hours now. She would stop breathing, journey off and then return with the terror of one who is starved for air. Her system was sending the equivalent of alarms and bells and whistles. *You are suffocating!* it would scream and she would return with a start, in fear for her life. I had no fear for her and it showed in my expression and demeanor. So I put my face in her path and it would be the first image she would catch sight of. My calm would then infuse her.

See, I knew in my heart that Ida was terrified of dying. I also knew that each trip she was making now was like a trial run and that my presence could melt the fear and ease her passing. And in so doing I earned many gifts. I got to see the wonder in her eyes as she returned and focusing on my gaze, love suffused her face. Sometimes, upon her re-emergence to consciousness, she would repeat the same sentence over and over. I began to see that many of these were unresolved concerns left over from long ago which had stayed with her. Others were stories or events of which she was proud and which she needed to share. And I was the vessel, the fortunate recipient of these gifts. Shya was as well, of course, for he was there in the room, but I loved being with Ida this way so he gave me space.

Clutching my hand, Ida lurched back to this reality. Disoriented for a minute, she tried to raise herself up to get more air. I am familiar with this feeling. It is not one of my favorites. Sometimes, while meaning to swallow, I actually inhale my spit instead and my throat closes; feeling as if I can't breathe, it is hard to relax and not panic. But relaxing was exactly what I was training Ida to do.

I am so pleased to see you back, my look said.

Her look had an intensity. *There is something I have to tell you,* it replied.

As I listened as intently as I knew how, she said, "You
have no idea what it is like to be dependent on money and then lose it. I <u>swore</u> I would <u>never</u> become dependent on money again!" There was a pleading in her eyes. *Don't judge me!* they entreated.

More pieces of the puzzle gently floated into place. Of course many families go through tight times and have to watch their pennies to make ends meet, but with Ida, conserving money had forever been a supreme priority. When Shya was 13, his older sister, Sandra, got a lump on her neck. "Just a swollen gland," the doctor said. For six months this "gland" stayed swollen and grew in size but no more trips to the doctor were scheduled, no second opinions asked for. Doctors cost money, after all. Finally, finally, they went again. But, by now, it was too late. Sandra had spinal cancer and she eventually succumbed to the disease, dying at age 24, seven long years later.

The decision to delay further action on Sandra's lump had embittered some family members but as I sat with this fragile old lady, holding her hand, I realized that at some moment in time when she was young, Ida had sworn to herself a solemn oath to conserve money, however large a sacrifice it might seem. She had made this promise to herself, never even glimpsing what the future might have in store, and she had paid the ultimate price.

"It's not right for a parent to outlive her children," she had told me more than once.

I smiled down at her a tender smile. *I love you. I forgive you. It's all right, you can rest now.*

Soon Ida began to slide in and out of consciousness with more and more ease. Today was not to be the day of her death, but it was coming. I could feel it.

Ten or so days later, Ida was again living in Intensive Care. She would not be going home again. But by now, Ida was bedridden. Hooked to an IV, with tubes of oxygen in her nose, she sucked air as she apologetically looked up at us, as if she was sorry to be causing so much trouble.

I was again in my customary spot by Ida's side, holding her hand. Within a few minutes, she started to drift in and out again, her breathing stopping, her neck pulsing, but by now the process was infinitely easier and simpler. Ida's eyes would remain open, her gaze fixed, and she would just go. When she came back, each return was new and fresh and alive. It went something like this:

As Ida regained awareness of her surroundings, Shya said, "Hello, Ida. Did you have a nice journey?"

"Oh yes," she replied with enthusiasm. "It was beautiful!"

She remained smiling, her wrinkled old face and sunken eyes beatific. Then her countenance relaxed and she was away again, her gaze still looking at me, but she was not there. Holding her hand, I waited. By now, Shya was sitting with me and we had our faces pressed side-by-side so she could see us both upon her re-emergence.

Sometimes she came back a bit disoriented but always, always she was so happy to see us.

"Oh, it's you!" she would exclaim. "I love you so much," and then she would go only to return again, surprised and delighted to see us once again, "Oh, it's you, I love you so much!" Each return was new. She was new and so were we.

At one point she became very lucid for a longer stretch of time. Taking Shya's hand, she gave him the equivalent of a dying sage's blessing.

"You know, I must admit, Shya, that when you were younger, I never thought you would turn out, but you did. I am very proud of you."

Wow, what a gift! We all cried as Shya and she held hands. Then she drifted away. Upon her return, Ida looked him in the eye and said, "You are going to be very famous some day," before she left again.

Ida was in a rhythm of her own now. She didn't need to be kept alive by us. Her body was closing itself down bit by bit. Her race was almost run.

Two nights later, she finally slipped away for good.

Ida was laid to rest in a beautiful mahogany casket that

Rhoda, Shya's sister, had picked out. Before the service, the family met.

It was a sad day. But, it was also a day where we shared stories about Ida Speiler who got married and became Ida Kane. These stories are a legacy which we preserved to be handed down to our children.

To get the ball rolling, Ida's only remaining sibling told a little of Ida's early life. Ruth, a tiny almost replica of her sister, stood and recited some facts of old that were new to us.

"Ida was born on Rivington Street near Delancey," she began. These streets are on Manhattan's Lower East Side.

"Things were pretty normal at first and then the Depression came. My father lost his job. Everyone was out of work and Ida got a job and supported the whole family. She was thirteen, then."

I got a rush as if someone had poured ice water over my head. The hairs raised on my arms. Of course. Now this puzzle was completed. I imagined a petite child of 13, laboring to feed her siblings and both parents. She had to support Harry, Eddy, Ruth, Matt, her mother, her father, and herself, seven in all.

"You have no idea what it is like to be dependent on money and then lose it." She had said, "I <u>swore</u> I would <u>never</u> become dependent on money again!"

Later during the service, I gave my own silent prayer, *Oh, Ida, Ida. I understand. I am so, so sorry. Things must have hurt really bad. I have such compassion for you. I love you so much. I hope now you can finally rest in peace.*

Ida was a beautiful, caring person whose actions had become twisted by the traumas to her heart. The decisions she made dictated her life and caused her and those around her great pain. But given the logic system that had evolved from her life circumstances, that was the only appropriate response she could see.

Our not judging her actions and holding them as "bad" allowed the resulting pain she felt to dissolve so that she could finally know peace, and so could we.

Awhile back, the two of us saw an episode of the television show, *Justice Files*. One segment of the program was the sentencing of a man who was convicted of the brutal rape and murder of a beautiful young girl. As part of the proceedings, members of the slain girl's family were allowed to stand up and address the defendant and judge so as to foster healing and closure for the bereaved. The girl's mother stood before the man who had just been sentenced to life in prison for killing her daughter and forgave him. The mother stated that she couldn't find it in her heart to hate him because if she did, that hatred would eat away at her heart. She forgave him and hoped that God would watch over him, wherever he went from there.

The person who is really freed when you forgive someone is you. Most people have no idea that their actions are held by you as transgressions so the person mainly punished when you hold a grudge, is you. Again, even if you are "correct", if you are being right about how another is wrong, something alive in you dies.

BIRTH OF THE PRESENT

ONCE YOU BEGIN TO FORGIVE PEOPLE AND EVENTS FROM YOUR past and let go of your history, the present begins to emerge. The approach or paradigm we are suggesting does not involve fixing your past or fixing your problems. This is confusing to most people because they naturally want to do something to make things better. They want a fix-it technique because they have the idea "the more you do, the more results you produce."

There is another paradigm called "being".

If you are being in this moment, all problems disappear automatically because problems are past-future oriented. All problems are a projection towards the future of possible realities based upon your past.

If you let go of the past and you let go of the future, there are no more problems. And it may sound glib to say this, but it really is true: The more willing you are to be here and let go of your history and your story, the more life can unfold in this moment.

Let's take a person with AIDS for example. We know a fellow for whom this affliction is a terrible torture. He is consumed with fears for what will come. It is a very painful experience.

We know another person whose contraction of the AIDS virus was a lifesaving gift. She is more alive than many "healthy" people could ever hope to be. She lives her life as though it were a gift to be savored, not worrying about possible futures but living moment to moment, appropriate to her needs. As she has become more aware, she naturally has started eating better and finding treatments which are effective for her.

This woman has no illusions about living forever, although she is very encouraged by new treatments which may keep the disease under control until there is a cure. But she is not merely gearing her life toward the future, hanging on for "better" days when she is cured. Rather, she is very alive right now. For this person, having the HIV virus is not an excuse for living in a diminished state.

84

THE PHILOSOPHER'S STONE

If you can stop blaming how you have turned out on your past, your life will magically transform. Forward and back, forever. Just by getting here now. As mentioned in the chapter on Instantaneous Transformation®, the philosopher's stone was something from ancient alchemy, the forerunner of chemistry, and it was purported to transmute base metals like lead into gold.

THERE IS A MODERN DAY PHILOSOPHER'S STONE

-- BEING IN THIS MOMENT --

AND WHAT IT DOES IS TRANSFORM ORDINARY, MUNDANE LIVES

INTO EXQUISITE, MAGNIFICENT LIVES

That's what's possible for everyone. It requires only one thing. It requires getting into the moment. Not thinking about the moment, not trying to change or fix any aspect of yourself.

There is no work involved in transformation. Transformation, as we said, is a state of being. It is a way to be in your life, and it isn't something that you do, like a practice. You can't *do* being transformed. You can *be* transformed.

85

When you are living in the moment, there is nothing you need to achieve, fix or get rid of and there is a deep sense of satisfaction that radiates from within rather than being just out of reach. When you are in the moment, what was once held as base becomes golden.

THE PRINCIPLES
OF TRANSFORMATION

THERE ARE THREE BASIC PRINCIPLES OF TRANSFORMATION.

The first principle is:

Anything you resist, persists -- and gets stronger.

You become attached to anything you push against. If you resist something, you become just like the thing you resist. Here is an example. Let's say that the fist represents your father, who you are resisting, and the open hand represents you. You push against your father because you resist him and pretty soon the open hand has assumed the shape of your father and you become just like him in the opposite. "Rebels" are not truly free. Because they define themselves in opposition to their parents or

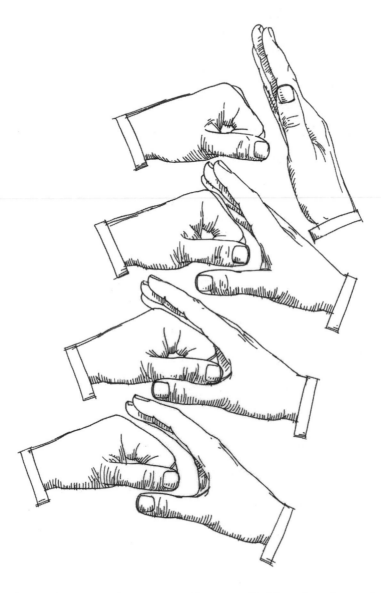

their upbringing, they are actually controlled by what they resist.

So, "anything you resist, persists" and sticks around.

If you want a more scientific explanation of this principle, it goes something like this: For every action there is an equal and opposite reaction.

The second principle is also a rule of physics:
No two things can occupy the same space at the same time.

For example, if a person is sitting in a chair, no other person can sit in that exact spot in that same chair at the exact same time.

In the case of emotions, you cannot be happy if you are actually sad -- no two emotions can occupy the exact same space at the exact same time.

The third principle is: Anything that you recreate or have be exactly as it is, will complete itself and disappear.

In other words, if you let things actually be the way they are, they disappear.

This includes psychological pain, physiological pain, emotional pain and upset. If you let yourself be upset when you are upset rather than trying to get rid of it (first principle: what you resist persists) then it will dissolve all on its own and disappear.

89

Have you noticed that happiness is fleeting? Do you resist it when it happens? Do you say, "Oh no, I'm happy again. I was hoping this happiness wouldn't overtake me"? Happiness is not one of those things we usually resist. So it goes really quickly. But if we're upset or sad, these states have a tendency to linger because we generally don't want to be upset when we are upset or sad when we are sad. Disagreeing with how your life is showing up in this moment is a form of resistance. And don't forget, resistance results in the unwanted condition's persistence.

Look at your life and see if everything that you have tried to get rid of, hasn't stuck around on some level. Those things that you push against, that you have said, "I have to change. I really shouldn't be like that," don't resolve. That's the first principle.

Again, the second principle is "No two things can occupy the same space at the same time." However, if you allow yourself to feel what you are feeling when you are feeling it, (this is the third principle) it will clear up and disappear.

Awareness, a non-judgmental investigation, can free you from old patterns -- even things that have gone on for years, that you've resisted, that you've tried to get rid of and have had New Year's resolutions about. If you allow yourself to be with anything, it loses its power over you. However, if you resist an old pattern of behavior, you give it power over your life.

We are suggesting a way of being that involves surrendering to your life, not resisting the way your life is showing up in each moment. Your life presents itself the way it does. It does not show up any differently. For instance, you can't be standing when you are sitting. Now, what you do with the way your life is showing up, is up to you.

Let's come back to the first principle. If you resist circumstances in your life, they persist. If on the other hand, you simply notice your circumstances, without judging what you see, if you just say, "Oh, this is the way my life is, OK," then unwanted patterns complete. However, you cannot "accept" something as a means to get rid of it, change it, or fix it. This is not acceptance at all. In actuality, acceptance with the agenda to change the situation is a manipulation to get to what you want rather than experiencing or being with what you have. Transformation doesn't work that way. But if you actually, genuinely choose to have what you have when you have it, it disappears.

OK. So, now you have the principles of transforma-   91
tion in a conceptual form. Perhaps you would like a practical example.

In 1982, when the two of us were on our third date, there was a dramatic incident in which the two of us had a first-hand experience that demonstrated the principles of transformation in action. The following story is told from Ariel's point of view.

THE BURN

It was a beautiful Sunday morning in late August and New York City seemed to be resting up for the week ahead. It was the kind of morning where you could see all the way up and down the avenues. What a glorious day for a ride to Jones Beach on the back of Shya's motorcycle, a Yamaha 650 Special, "Old Blue". We had bundled our towels and sunscreen behind the seat and, thus prepared, headed out of town.

It felt like flying. We were both dressed in shorts and T-shirts, our heads protected by helmets and visors, and the morning sun felt good on my skin. What an excellent day to be alive! Even the traffic lights seemed to be going our way.

Shortly after we breezed through the tunnel into Queens, we took an exit and made our way to an open gas station. Pulling up to the pump, Shya stood Old Blue on the kickstand and opened the tank to fill it up.

Deciding to stretch my legs, I began to step off the bike when I felt a sharp, searing pain. Jumping with a yelp, I looked down at my left calf. What I saw was a raw patch with a piece of melted skin hanging off. Unwittingly, I had placed my leg squarely against the hot muffler. I was dumbfounded.

Staring at my injury, I slowly stated the obvious, "I guess I burned my leg."

Just one glance told Shya the whole story and sent him into action.

"Ice!"

The station didn't have any so Shya sprinted off in an attempt to locate some. But there wasn't even a corner store or local coffee shop open for business. Stuffing a five in the hand of the attendant, we rushed to make our way to Jones Beach, which seemed the closest alternative for ice. The wind on the burn was wicked. The air that had only moments before seemed to spell freedom now brought fire with its touch. The shock of the initial injury having worn off, I was now crying freely as I held Shya tightly around the middle and we sped to the beach.

By the time we pulled into the parking lot, I was beside myself in pain. Pulling up to the curb, Shya hopped off and grabbing our things, he gave me a hand as I limped over to a nearby concession stand where surely they had ice and some cooling relief.

I stood shakily nearby, almost mute with pain, and Shya ran up to the nearest person behind the counter.

"Quick, I need some ice. My girlfriend has been badly burned!"

I turned to show her my leg, which by now looked white and red and raw, thoroughly seared and nauseating to look

93

at. Sometimes when I see a person with a particularly nasty looking abrasion, I get a sensation that shoots into my stomach or
groin as I can imagine the pain. Had I been a casual observer, I
am sure the sight of my leg would have brought a similar rush.

In one fluid movement the manager scooped a large cup
of ice and said, "Sorry about your leg. Be sure to come back if
you need more."

Wrapping the cubes in a napkin, I hesitantly pressed the
cold to my injury. The touch of the paper was agonizing and I
realized I was shaking. As the ice began to melt, dripping down
my leg, I finally found some numbing comfort.

Eventually, Shya and I shared a plate of greasy French
fries and ketchup, and I realized that I wasn't going to get to lay
on my towel and sun myself that day. The idea of sand on my calf
made me cringe. So we sat at the table, people watching and sip-
ping a giant Coke and looking at the tantalizing ocean in the distance as we waited for the chill to take over and quiet the fiery
spot on my left calf.

Finally, with the pain mostly under control, we decided

to cut our losses and head for home. I refilled my napkin with bits of ice for the ride back to the city and we began to make our way to the parking lot and our trusty steed, Old Blue, who was stoically awaiting our return.

There was only one problem with this plan. By the time we had gotten to the bike, the pain in my leg had reflared ten-fold and each stride had become agonizing as the calf muscle flexed and bunched under the wound with each step. It felt as if the skin was drying and cracking and the throbbing, which had mostly been held at bay by the icy compresses, began to pound in earnest.

I sat down on the curb by the bike, pressed the compress to my leg, laid my head on my knees and began to cry. I could tell my shoulders were lurching up and down with my sobs but they couldn't be controlled any more than the intense throbbing was being controlled by the meager amount of ice I had left in the napkin. Just the idea of wind rushing across the open sore on the way home was enough to cause my sobs to deepen.

Shya sat beside me and took my free hand in his. Gently, his voice came in my ear, "Ariel, let's look at the pain together."

"NO! Don't touch it!" I cried, hunching protectively over the leg.

"Ariel," he continued quietly, "I don't want to touch it. Let's just examine the pain. OK?"

Hesitantly, I raised my head. I looked into his intense eyes and slowly nodded as the tears streamed down my face.

"Trust me," he said.

As I gazed into his eyes, I had no doubt that I could trust this man. There was a calm in him -- a steadiness which seemed to translate itself to me. It calmed some of the hysteria of my sobs into sniffles and hiccups, but the tears still silently slid down my cheeks because while I wished I could crawl out of my skin and leave it behind, the pain in my leg was very real and agonizing and no amount of wishing it would be different seemed to change the situation.

"Ready?" he asked. I nodded and so we began.

I didn't know at the time that we were going to perform

magic. All I knew is that we were going to look at the pain, whatever that meant.

"OK, Ariel. Close your eyes and look at the pain with your mind's eye. If the pain in your calf had a color, what color would it be?"

That was easy. "Fiery red."

"Fine. Now, if it could hold water, how much water would it hold?"

I pictured in a flash the swimming pool from my Alma Mater, Mt. Hood Community College, so I told Shya it would hold as much water as "an Olympic-sized swimming pool."

"OK," he said "How about now? If it had a shape what shape would it be?"

"Flat, kind of oval with rough and bumpy razor sharp edges sticking out."

"Good, Ariel. You are doing just fine. Take a look at the pain now and on a scale of ten, ten being excruciating and zero being no pain, what number does the pain in your leg have now?"

"23!"

I knew the number I gave him was off the scale but I didn't care. My leg hurt and it hurt darn bad.

"All right. And if it had a color right now, Ariel, what color would it be?"

As I looked the color had changed. It was now an orangey red with flaring spots of more intense color and so that is what I reported. As the process continued, Shya kept directing me to look at the shape and color and number and volume of water the spot on my leg held now and now and now. Each moment became a separate jewel in time. Not to be gotten away from or ignored -- Nor to be compared to the moment preceding it -- They became individual facets to be investigated and described.

As I looked an amazing thing happened. The color changed through yellows to blues and greens, and finally turned white. The volume of water shrank, to a gallon, quart, cup and eventually was only to be measured in teaspoons and then drops. Even as the shape shrank to be the size of the head of a pin, so did the numbers I assigned to the pain's intensity recede to two and then one.

99

We had done it! We had looked at the pain of the situation squarely in the eye and it had disappeared, dissolved, transformed. I felt a profound sense of relief. And it wasn't just a parlor trick either. Gingerly, I got up and walked a bit. The pain had somehow been lifted even more than when it had been chilled by two giant soft drink cups worth of ice. And the sensation didn't even flare up on the ride home, even with the wind wrapping itself around my leg.

EACH MOMENT BECAME A SEPARATE JEWEL IN TIME. NOT TO BE GOTTEN AWAY FROM OR IGNORED -- NOR TO BE COMPARED TO THE MOMENT PRECEDING IT -- THEY BECAME INDIVIDUAL FACETS TO BE INVESTIGATED AND DESCRIBED

Looking again at the principles of transformation in this situation, what we did was:

1. Not resist what was, i.e., the pain or the fact that Ariel had been burned.

The concept most people hold about pain is that it is static and always the same. This is inaccurate.

2. We looked at the pain moment-by-moment to see the truth of it in each moment and recognize the pain could only be the way it was.

3. By actually letting the pain be the way it was, it completed itself and disappeared.

HAPPINESS

FROM THE TIME WE WERE CHILDREN, WE HAVE absorbed the idea that it is better to be happy. Everyone knows it is better to be happy and joyous than sad and angry or upset and unsure of what to do with one's life. So people try to be happy.

In the United States we pursue "The American Dream". We have been taught that landing the right job or acquiring certain possessions will bring satisfaction. And of course, many believe that finding that perfect someone, our soul mate, will bring eternal bliss. Obviously, this isn't true. How many of us have found the relationship of our dreams only to have it turn into a nightmare?

Remember how excited you were when you got that doll or toy or your favorite hero on a baseball card? And later how it felt to finally get your first car or stereo system or that engagement ring? Today those toys and possessions are long since discarded, forgotten, or taken for granted in your day-to-day life. Especially those of us who have been very good at acquiring things have discovered that this form of happiness is transitory at best.

Some have found their "soul mate" only to keep wondering why other areas of their lives aren't working and wondering if maybe there is more to life than just a great relationship. It wasn't too long ago that having a family was going to do it -- yet these days, the cat is out of the bag -- raising a child is hard work and stressful at times, too.

So what are we to do? It seems as if our myths and superstitions which were purported to be the signposts for utopia are being discarded along the road. Yet most of us are left with the same question which sings to us, repeating like variations on a theme throughout our lives:

How can I achieve true and lasting happiness in this lifetime?

The two of us, after much searching and working on ourselves, pushing and prodding, stumbled into something which has led to an ongoing sense of satisfaction and well-being -- a state which *includes* happiness as well as the entire range of human emotions. We have found this moment and in so doing have found the answer to that age-old quest for lasting fulfillment and satisfaction. True and lasting happiness can only be found now, in this moment.

Part of the reason most people's lives are not happy is that they have designated "happy" as a desired state and then they resist or judge those states that are not. This locks them into the emotion or condition which they are resisting.

UNTIL YOU ARE WILLING TO BE THE WAY YOU ARE

-- IN ANY GIVEN MOMENT --

YOU CAN NEVER BE HAPPY

BECAUSE HAPPINESS IS ONLY ONE

OF MANY EMOTIONS THAT HUMAN BEINGS

ARE CAPABLE OF EXPERIENCING

If we resist whatever emotion happens to be there in this moment in favor of a preferred emotion, i.e., happiness, we are stuck with the emotion we are resisting. For example, if you only like sunny weather and then a cloud bank comes along, you are likely to resist it, spending time and energy trying to stop the clouds, rather than let them move through. Your efforts to regain the sunny times actually keep the sky in perpetual rainy weather. How many times have you seen somebody smiling and you can see that while pretending to be happy they are actually in pain? They are upset.

What we are saying is, if you are willing to experience what is happening in your life in this moment, it will allow the situation to ease. For instance, if you are experiencing sadness and you don't resist it and you don't try to get rid of it and you don't try to be happy instead, but just let yourself feel the emotion of sadness, it will complete itself.

105

Most people's lives are about avoiding those experiences or emotions that they consider negative. When these "negative" experiences or emotions are avoided and we try to live our lives pretending they don't exist, they persist as current themes and no amount of achievement or acquiring or cosmetic surgery will change that. So we become prisoners of an attempt to avoid unpleasant experiences in our lives in favor of "happiness".

The essence of true happiness comes out of your willingness to experience what is between you and happiness. Most people are not willing to do that, so they have to settle for a pale facsimile. But you can't be with sadness in order to get over it, for that is not being with it at all. That is just an attempt to manipulate yourself so that you can once again achieve what your mind says is going to make you happy.

Have you ever been with a people who are truly sad? We are not talking about wallowing around, feeling sorry for themselves or dramatizing the emotion so that they don't have to feel, but people who are actually allowing themselves to touch into a deep well of sadness or grief, perhaps over the passing of a loved one. Or perhaps you have been with someone as he or she have been close to death. Being with someone in this state is rich. It is alive. It can be healing and surprisingly, it can feel wonderful. Sometimes it is in these moments that people discover how to truly be intimate -- they rediscover their ability to love and have compassion.

ONLY BY BEING THE WAY YOU ARE

CAN YOU FIND

THAT ELUSIVE STATE OF CONTENTMENT

W.O.R.M.S
WRITE ONCE READ MANY

THE DECISIONS THAT WE MADE EARLY IN OUR LIVES OFTEN remain unchallenged and forgotten. Have you considered that your internal dialogue may actually be a collection of ancient recordings that have no real relevance to this moment?

It has been said that we have approximately 187,000 thoughts a day, 98% of which we had the day before and the day before that. People's minds operate in a similar manner to a tape recorder on playback, feeding us old information as if it is brand new.

The commentary about your life that plays inside the privacy of your own thoughts is like a bright penny hung on a string. Sometimes the string rotates one way and the light of the day catches your penny and you think to yourself that you are doing pretty good. Other times your thoughts twist the other direction, illuminating the idea that what you are doing is no good at all or that nothing you do will ever really make a difference. Most of us are mesmerized by that twisting and turning penny. We love it when it gyrates in the direction that praises our strengths and bemoan the times when it swings back to those old self-deprecating thoughts. If you want to live in a truly satisfying manner, it is essential to take your attention off the lure of that bright penny, off your compelling internal commentary -- whether it be for or against your current circumstances.

Your mind operates like a computer. In computer technology there is an acronym for a type of data storage called a W.O.R.M. which stands for: Write Once Read Many. It is a system for permanently keeping information. The data is indelibly written and can never be altered. It is then available to be read, as though new, as many times as you want.

Our minds too, are full of W.O.R.M.s. In moments of stress or contraction or times when our survival seems threatened, we make decisions to avoid repeating those things that we think caused the crisis. Decisions, even those made long ago, are stored in your mind in such a way that you can read them many times as though brand new and true in this moment, applicable to your current circumstances.

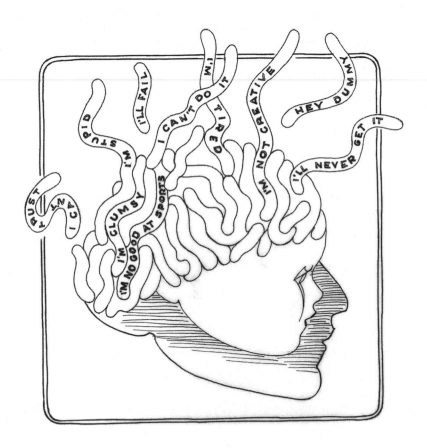

Once these decisions are written (stated to ourselves), they are held as truths over time in our minds. Then when a current situation in your environment is similar to a time when that decision was made, your mind accesses the W.O.R.M. and it plays back as if it is totally new information.

Here's an example of how it works. Let's say little Billy was called upon to answer a question at school. He thought he had the right answer but when he said it out loud it was wrong. The other kids laughed and in Billy's mind, even the teacher seemed to be making fun of him. Billy then hunched his shoulders, slid lower in his seat and said to himself...

Here is the start of a W.O.R.M. In this case it happened when Billy didn't like what he was feeling and when he wanted to avoid the discomfort again. The logic system is something like: "Yuk, I didn't like that. I don't want that to happen again. Maybe it is better to say I don't know, even if I do. Then I won't have to risk being laughed at and humiliated again." So Billy sets in place the beginning of a life strategy, but he forgets he made that decision. Then as an adult, Bill wonders why he is so tentative in business meetings. He is frustrated that ideas and answers always seem to be on the tip of his tongue but other people always seem to be faster at expressing them and they get the credit, not he.

Here are some sample W.O.R.M.s. Are any of yours in here?

I will never let that happen again.

I'll never be like them.

I won't let myself be vulnerable again.

I can't trust men.

I can't trust women.

I'll never be successful, why try?

I am not attractive.

I'm done with dating.

I'm not creative.

I'm no good at sports.

I'm not intellectual enough.

I'm stupid.

I'm tired.

I can't do it.

Money is hard to come by.

No matter what I do it's not good enough.

I'm clumsy.

I'm no good with my hands.

They don't like me because I am too... small, big, fat, skinny, old, young, poor, rich, short, tall, uneducated, overqualified, nice, mean, etc.

There are, conservatively speaking, a million other W.O.R.M.s but for the sake of brevity we will leave the list short.

Sometimes W.O.R.M.s are not only thought processes but emotions. Take the person who used to cry as a child, when caught doing something "bad". Because he or she was already upset, the parent didn't have the heart to administer punishment. Thus the child learns to survive via tears. Now as an adult, whenever things get pressured or mistakes are made at work, tears spring unbidden to his or her eyes. Write Once Read Many. As an adult, you may not appreciate some of these reflexive, mechanical behaviors but many of these ways of being and relating worked once for us when we were younger. They were recorded and then the mind replays them as strategic moves and our lives are an endless repetition of the past.

When there is a lapse in activity, or when under stress, your mind will go to a familiar conversation by default much in the same way a computer has a screen saver that fills your monitor with messages or images of flying toasters. Perhaps the "I'm still hungry" or "I can't handle this, I'm out of here!" message is no more current or serious than a toaster with wings except that you forgot you were listening to an old recording.

It is easy to be fooled, though. At least with a phono-graph, we can hear the telltale scratchy sounds of old time record-ing techniques. However, with your own personal, mental W.O.R.M.s, they get more sophisticated and polished as you do. Kind of an automatic, courtesy upgrade.

DECISIONS

If physicists are accurate, then the universe is always expanding. If you make a rule to live by, then it has to be limiting even if the basic premise was sound. Therefore, simply by living out of a decision you are destined to be an inhibited, fettered version of yourself.

It is akin to buying a little potted sapling and taking it out to the forest where the ground is fertile and where it will get just the right amount of sunshine, rain and wind. But, when you plant the tree, you leave it in its original pot and plant it container and all. The pot then defines how far the tree can grow. It acts as a boundary that determines how deep the roots can reach and therefore how high its limbs can climb. The pot, our decisions, effectively stunt our ability to grow and we become root bound, stagnant in our lives.

It is important to differentiate between deciding and choosing. Please don't get caught up in the words being used here. It is not our intention to get the readers of this book to manipulate their language so that they are now speaking in a new and improved system where using the word "choice" is better than "decision". Rather, see if you can catch the distinction between the two so that you are empowered in your life. It may be a bit confusing at first and seem to be primarily an exercise in semantics. However, the difference between the essence of what we will term decision and choice may hold the key to your discovery of Self-Satisfaction.

DECISIONS - VS - CHOICES

Let's look at the differences between decisions and choices. A decision is intellectually determined, based upon your considerations. A choice, on the other hand, is a selection made after consideration that is reflective of your heartfelt desires or authentic wishes. So in other words, when you decide something, you weigh the pros and the cons, basically making two columns where you add up the arguments for and against an action. Depending on which has more weight, you follow the prescribed course. A choice, however, takes all of those pros and cons into account, but once all of the information is examined it allows for intuitive leaps, heartfelt moves, and creative alternatives that might not have been suggested by mere factual analysis and simple deductive reasoning. Decisions are reasonable whereas choices, while including logic, are not based solely in reasons.

CHOICES ARE THE EXPRESSION OF YOUR HEART

A DECISION IS THE MANDATE OF A W.O.R.M.

At very best, decisions we make and follow are made by a younger, less sophisticated version of ourselves. Would you seriously ask a 2 or 3 year old what you should do with your life and then live out of that advice? Yet this is essentially what many of us have done. We live out of the decisions reached by our minds when we were very young.

It is kind of like a squirrel who gets caught in the middle of the road in the path of an onrushing vehicle. This animal doesn't know which direction to go for safety and in its terror it scurries back and forth, helter-skelter in jerky little movements and a rush of adrenaline. Luckily, the car or truck happens to miss crushing the animal. But now, the squirrel has filed this behavior as a survival strategy. It was coincidental that the squirrel didn't get flattened. Its life was saved in spite of its remaining in the roadway. Our minds work in the same manner. They record all of the data, even the coincidental information, sometimes linking the two. Usually we don't realize that we achieve goals or move forward in our lives in spite of the self-deprecating thought patterns and self reproaches that were mistakenly linked as an integral part of our survival.

117

"Are all decisions made in a moment of contraction?" you might ask. The answer is yes. Let's say you do something that is "right" and you get rewarded or recognized. While basking in the good feelings you say, "Wow, this really worked. I am going to keep doing that!" But this decision is already based on the idea that you can't trust yourself in the future to make the right choices which will produce the good feelings again. The mind wants to systematize what it thinks you did right as well as what it thinks you did wrong in order to assure your survival. And perhaps a good portion of the time this survival strategy may be sound, but sooner or later doing anything by rote will get you in trouble. Repeating even "good" moves gets tedious because it cuts out the possibility of new, creative solutions.

So how does one recognize when a seemingly current choice is just an old W.O.R.M.? There are some telltale signs that will help you recognize when you are authentically expressing yourself as opposed to when you are stuck in the groove of an old, but perhaps not so favorite song.

118

ODDLY ENOUGH, SOMETIMES WHAT YOU DECIDE TO DO AND

WHAT YOU WOULD CHOOSE TO DO MAY BE THE SAME

THERE IS, HOWEVER, A VAST CONTRAST

IN THE EXPERIENCE OF SATISFACTION

DEPENDING ON THE ROUTE YOU TAKE

TO YOUR FINAL DESTINATION

You can really see the difference in two individuals' approaches to goals. One has decided that the life he or she has now is not good enough and plans to get a new job, relationship or buy something to fix the problem. This is a problem/solution framework that does not lead to satisfaction. When this person reaches a goal, there may be a momentary feeling of victory but that sense of dissatisfaction is still lurking around the corner. Then come the "what ifs" and self doubts and the pattern starts all over again once the pressure of life builds.

The other individual may have the same goals as the first. But even if the actions taken to achieve results are similar, if not coming out of the context that something is wrong or deficient with him or her, then each step of the journey can be fulfilling and exciting. When the second individual reaches a goal, it is simply an extension of the profound satisfaction which he or she is already experiencing.

Another indicator of being in the grips of a W.O.R.M. is something that could be called the "déjà-vu factor". This is the feeling you get when you are poised to say the thing you know will get you into a fight but can't seem to help doing it. Or it is when you are upset at something or someone in your current environment but it is the same old feeling you have had many, many times before.

If you are making a life move and are defensive about it you can be sure there is a decision in there somewhere. A choice is not defendable. How can you adequately explain or prove intuitive hunches or knowing something in your heart?

So, how do we get rid of the W.O.R.M.s that we have made? Here is the good news and the bad news: We can't. Don't forget what W.O.R.M. stands for: Write Once Read Many. These decisions are set in place and available to be read forever. However, you can bypass them, and awareness is the key. If you notice your behavior, like a modern day anthropologist, it will allow you to disengage from old decisions. What it takes is neutral observation without punishing, chastising or even congratulating yourself for what you see.

IF YOU QUESTION, LOOK AT
AND EXAMINE YOUR THOUGHTS
WITHOUT JUDGING WHAT YOU FIND
IT IS ENOUGH TO DISSOLVE
THE MECHANICAL NATURE OF YOUR LIFE

You basically have two options: whether to operate through old decisions or to look freshly at your life and see what it is that you want to do from your heart and your truth, rather than from an old agenda. Don't worry if you have made decisions or choices in the past. Everyone has done his or her share of both. Second guessing yourself can easily lead to the creation of a whole new set of decisions.

In fact, after reading this chapter, you could decide to not make decisions any more -- you are only going to make choices because choices are better. Ahh, the mind is tricky.

THE ATTAINMENT OF GOALS & SATISFACTION

Folks are waiting to be saved from their current state or circumstances by a blinding flash of insight, or perhaps on a less esoteric level by winning the lottery. They want to graduate to their idea of what it means to have arrived, to have achieved success and be truly an adult. In spiritual vernacular this means we feel we should have become "enlightened" by now and nothing should ever cause us to fall off center, be upset or ill again. Satisfaction, however, is not circumstantially determined.

People have the false belief that if only they had perfect health or had the right job, the right boyfriend or girlfriend, the right toys to play with, then they would be satisfied. Yet there are doctors who find doctoring boring and frustrating. There are teachers who are just waiting to retire. There are people who have everything money can buy but all their gadgets and gizmos give them no pleasure. Others are certain they have found that special someone and yet even another's love can't fill the void.

If you are satisfied, you bring your satisfaction to the moment and fill the circumstances of your life with that satisfaction. If you are dissatisfied, however, no one and nothing can produce contentment for you. If you listen to your internal commentary in regards to your likes and dislikes, it will prevent you from experiencing a satisfied life. In *hsin hsin ming* written 1400 years ago by the third Zen patriarch, Sengtsan, it says, "To set up what you like against what you dislike is the disease of the mind."

How often are tasks left unfinished simply because we do not like to do them, yet these incompletions plague us throughout our days? How often is our sleep disturbed by thoughts of incomplete projects or events that happened which weren't to our liking?

MOST OF US LIVE IN A CONSTANT STATE
OF COMPLAINT

Our internal conversation or dialogue, the voice we listen to that we attach our name to and believe to be us, is constantly complaining and nattering about how what is going on in
our lives is wrong -- how it should be different or better than it
is. This habituated way of interacting with our lives has been
passed down to us from generation to generation. As infants, the
way we learned was to absorb the culture that we found ourselves
in. This is why everybody who was raised in the South has a
southern accent and everyone who was raised in New England
sounds like a "Yankee".

Enlightenment, satisfaction, waking up, happens when
you interact with your life as though you are doing exactly what
you are supposed to be doing and your circumstances are exactly what they are supposed to be rather than complaining about
your life. This state of enlightenment is not elusive. What it
requires is getting here and now. It is simple. Deceptively simple. So simple that it is difficult to understand.

It is possible for you right now, given your current cir-
cumstance, to discover your state of being as enlightened. In fact,
the only way to realize enlightenment is to have the current circumstances that you have in your life in this moment.

124

Accepting, allowing and interacting with your life as though it is exactly as it should be, without making yourself wrong (or right) for what you discover is the way to Self-Realization. The way to enlightenment is to reveal to yourself, honestly, the ways in which you are mechanically interacting with your life and not try to do something about it or change it. "What!" you might say, "don't change it?" Yes, Self-Realization lies in awareness and not in a problem/solution framework.

RESISTANCE TO THE CIRCUMSTANCES
OF YOUR LIFE
PERPETUATES DISSATISFACTION
AND GENERATES PAIN

Awareness, as we have said, is a state of being, not doing. If you become aware of a behavior pattern, the simple awareness of that pattern is enough to transform it. If you do something to change the pattern, it will perpetuate it. We are not suggesting that there aren't things that must be done in our daily lives. Awareness can include doing. This concept is illustrated in a story about a master and his disciple who were traveling through the desert. One evening they came to an oasis where they bedded down for the night. When they awoke in the morning, however, their camels were gone. Since tethering the camels each night was the disciple's responsibility, the master asked him whether he had secured them for the night. The disciple replied, "No master. You teach that we should trust in Allah. I was trusting that Allah would take care of the camels for us." To this his master responded, "Yes, trust in Allah, but you must also tether the camels."

When you are aware, you act appropriately, doing what is needed and wanted. These actions aren't born of a decision to do it right. They won't be reflective of your agenda to "do better next time". Your actions, the things you do, become authentic expressions of your True Self rather than the execution of something you have decided to do in an attempt to be a "better" you. To decide (same root as suicide and homicide) is similar to being "dead right"; both kill off the alternatives.

Awareness results in erasure or completion if that awareness is non-judgmental and without preference. Sengtsan, the author of *hsin hsin ming*, also said that "The Great Way is not difficult for those who have no preferences." It is your preferences which are socially conditioned. It is those same preferences that come into play when things don't go the way you think they should. If you invest in being right about what you would prefer then you generate pain and dissatisfaction and all creativity comes to a halt. A simple noting that things are different than what you would prefer -- and the way is open again. Contrary to popular belief, acceptance does not lead to complacency. Actually it empowers the individual to become responsive rather than reactive. While it is true that this day and age brings challenges and changes that our ancestors never had to consider, it is also true that some ideas can endure the test of time:

THE GREAT WAY

The Great Way is not difficult
for those who have no preferences.
When love and hate are both absent
everything becomes clear and undisguised.
Make the smallest distinction, however,
and heaven and earth are set infinitely apart.
If you wish to see the truth
then hold no opinions for or against anything.
To set up what you like against what you dislike
is the disease of the mind.

From Sengtsan's, *hsin hsin ming*

ACKNOWLEDGMENTS

THIS BOOK HAS BEEN A LABOR OF LOVE, NOT ONLY BY THE TWO OF US, but also by many, many talented friends who have unselfishly supported us along the way. We are grateful to and thank all of those who have ever graced us with their presence in one of our seminars or consulting sessions. We deeply appreciate all of those who have listened to or read the various incarnations of our manuscript and gave us feedback and encouragement. That being said, we would like to thank specifically many of those who so richly deserve praise.

First, Judith Service Montier, who by setting up our very first workshop in New York, launched our careers and introduced us to two of our closest friends, Josh and Laura Blau. Not only does Josh manage our finances and Laura take care of our contracts, etc., but they have also been incredible confidants, proofreaders, sounding boards and best of pals. Thanks guys - we couldn't have done it without you.

Other important people are John Lehman, who hosted our early seminars at his voice studio in Manhattan's West Village and who has now introduced us to an incredible group of people in Germany, Clardy Malugen, who came up with the phrase, Instantaneous Transformation® and Stephanie Teuwen, who was smart enough to suggest we trademark it. Steve Stein started us down the road to so many things: the expo circuit, the world of audio tapes and ultimately to Bali, Indonesia where we now have built an exquisite Conference Center. Bill Sayler, Shya's oldest friend, trusted us enough to unleash us on his business at the start of our careers and whose challenges with his parents' failing health inspired us to write the "Ida" chapter.

Mac and Ellen Jackson took our work to the next level and introduced us to the corporate world.

Tamara Pomert and Isabelle Soudrie, we appreciate your meticulous transcriptions of our taped events, transforming our spoken words into written ones so that we could weave the information into the fabric of this book. Geert Teuwen, we owe you for the many hours spent on the layout as well as for our photo on the back cover. John DeLillo for the sumptuous and fragrant meals you made which sustained us during our marathon editing and design sessions. Helene DeLillo for the incredible cover art -- and you truly are an artist. Our brother-in-law, Barney (Barnett Plotkin) whose brilliant illustrations have added whole new dimensions to our book -- We'll have to write another just to have the opportunity to work with you again!

Catherine Wayland, you came on board at the perfect time and we value your enthusiasm and support. Thanks also to Amy and Andrew Gideon who introduced us to the World Wide Web and who have designed and maintained our website. You and your staff at TAG Online have taken a daunting medium and made it easy and accessible for us.

We are also grateful to White Pine Press of Fredonia, NY for graciously allowing us to reprint the excerpt of *hsin hsin ming*.

These acknowledgments would not be complete without thanking Paul English, Publisher and Editor of Free Spirit Magazine which is home to our column, "In the Moment". Writing for you taught us that we could do it. Thanks also for suggesting "Working on Yourself Doesn't Work" as the title for this book.

Last but not least, we are very thankful to Brett and Mary Yeager, a beautiful couple who pushed and prodded, encouraged and faithfully told us the truth and without whom we are certain *Working on Yourself Doesn't Work* would still be a dream and not a reality.

ARIEL & SHYA KANE –
BEING IN THE MOMENT AUDIO TAPES SERIES

Instantaneous Transformation®

When you hear Ariel and Shya Kane's "Instantaneous Transformation®" audio workshop, it could dramatically change your life. The Kanes have found that the slightest shift in one's reality can produce a quantum shift in one's life. When that instant occurs, it is hard to say. You just suddenly realize that you feel lighter, freer, more alive and that you are interacting naturally and effectively with your present environment.

By listening to these two unique tapes, you can discover fulfillment without working on yourself.
Audio Cassettes – $16.95 1hr 48min

Instantaneous Transformation®
An Honest Look at Self-Realization
with Ariel & Shya Kane

"Listening to this tape may be the only workshop you ever need to experience." Dayna Cole, NAPRA ReVIEW

Completing Your Karma

ARIEL & SHYA KANE
Being In The Moment Series

If you are looking to dramatically expand your experience of well-being and wish to live an exciting, fun and extraordinary life, this series of audio tapes is for you!

Completing Your Karma

This compelling audio will help you to discover how to neutralize and dissolve "karma", the lingering ill effects from earlier mechanical ways of relating and behaving. Join the Kanes in this lively discussion which opens the door to living in the moment. This highly effective workshop outlines the keys to maximizing productivity and satisfaction. As you, too, complete your own personal karma, you will naturally have a less stressful attitude toward previously distressing situations, and a strengthened ability to be present in the moment, regardless of the circumstances.
Audio Cassettes – $16.95 1hr 23min

The Principles of Transformation

In these cassettes you will learn the three fundamental principles that will facilitate personal transformation.

During this extraordinary seminar, the Kanes reveal a revolutionary new technology that will allow you to reach a state of awareness and centeredness that in the past took many years to achieve. Listen to these audios and master the Principles of Transformation which will produce a quantum shift in your ability to be effective, productive and lead a highly satisfying life.
Audio Cassettes – $16.95 2hr 26min

The Principles of Transformation

ARIEL & SHYA KANE
Being In The Moment Series

If you are looking to dramatically expand your experience of well-being and wish to live an exciting, fun and extraordinary life, this series of audio tapes is for you!

Magical Relationships™

Since their first date in 1982 and subsequent marriage in 1984, Ariel and Shya have discovered that there are fundamental elements for finding a relationship, and keeping it alive, exciting and new. At this special event, taped live in New York City, the Kanes discuss the essence of creating Magical Relationships™. By listening to this audio, you will learn the keys that are of vital importance for getting 'em, having 'em and keeping 'em.

Whether you are searching for that special someone or already have found the person of your dreams, these cassettes will reveal how to have truly Magical Relationships™.
Audio Cassettes - $16.95 1hr 51min

More... Magical Relationships™

Ariel and Shya Kane's Magical Relationships™ audio was so powerful, that people wanted More...
- so here it is!

By listening to these audios, you will learn more of the keys that are of vital importance for having all of your relationships be exciting, fresh and satisfying.

This tape expands upon the principles of the Kanes' dramatic new technology, Instantaneous Transformation®, in a way that you, too, can discover how to truly have Magical Relationships™.
Audio Cassettes - $16.95 1hr 48min

The Roots of Satisfaction

By listening to this dynamic audio you will discover in yourself, the "Roots of Satisfaction". You will learn to recognize and bypass the most common obstacles and misconceptions that get in the way of your self-fulfillment. You will also find out how to access and experience a state of well-being where life unfolds naturally and produces a profound sense of satisfaction.

As they answer questions and interact with people with surprising ease, gentleness and candor, Ariel and Shya guide you on the path to your self-discovery.
Audio Cassettes - $16.95 1hr 22min

For articles, further titles, a schedule of Ariel & Shya's current seminars or to order online via secure server, visit the Kanes' website: www.ask-inc.com

Send Orders To:
ASK Productions, Inc.
PMB 137
208 East 51st Street
New York, NY 10022-6500
or
via Secure Order Form at
http://www.ask-inc.com

Books:

☞ **Working on Yourself Doesn't Work** ___ x $12.95

Audios:

☞ **Instantaneous Transformation®** ___ x $16.95
☞ **Completing Your Karma** ___ x $16.95
☞ **The Principles of Transformation** ___ x $16.95
☞ **Magical Relationships™** ___ x $16.95
☞ **More... Magical Relationships™** ___ x $16.95
☞ **The Roots of Satisfaction** ___ x $16.95

Payable in U.S. funds only. No cash/COD accepted. Postage & handling: U.S./CAN.
$4.00 for 1 - 3 tapes/books. $7.00 for 4 - 8 tapes/books. $1.00 for each additional item.
We accept Visa, MC, check and money orders.

Bill my: ❑ Visa ❑ MC _____(Expiration Date)
Card#_____
Name as it appears on Card_____
Signature_____

Billing Name & Address:
Name_____
Address_____
City_____
State, Zip_____
Daytime Phone#_____
Ship to:
Name_____
Address_____
City_____
State, Zip_____

Tape/Book Total $_____
NJ 6% or NY 8.25%
Sales Tax When Applicable $_____
Postage & Handling $_____
Total Amount Due $_____

This offer subject to change without notice.

OTHER OFFERINGS BY THE KANES

SEMINARS:

INSTANTANEOUS TRANSFORMATION®EVENINGS

These evenings are exciting explorations which open the door to living in the moment. Each session is a unique impromptu event formed by the interests and questions of those who attend. Not just an introduction to the work of Ariel and Shya Kane, they are actual opportunities for people to discover their ability to relate effectively and experience satisfaction in all areas of their lives.

MAGICAL RELATIONSHIPS™: HOW TO GET 'EM, HOW TO HAVE 'EM & HOW TO KEEP 'EM

Since their first date in 1982 and subsequent marriage in 1984, Ariel and Shya have discovered that there are specific keys to finding a relationship and keeping it alive, exciting and new. Whether you are searching for someone or already have found the person of your dreams, this workshop reveals how to truly have Magical Relationships™.

INTUITION

Do you remember what it was like when you were a kid and you knew things but you couldn't explain how you knew them? We have been taught that this natural knowing doesn't really exist, and that you have to figure things out or have reasonable explanations for how you know what you know. There are phenomena which cannot be explained this way: psychic abilities, foreseeing the future, seeing people's past and reading their thoughts. In a light and fun way, this workshop explores these realms. It includes a series of exercises and experiments designed to allow you to discover your own natural abilities to access your intuition and creativity.

TRANSFORMATIONAL TIME & PROJECT MANAGEMENT

In this course, participants learn how to effectively and effortlessly complete projects and tasks. This fun and lively interactive seminar will inspire you to see projects in a whole new way and have quantum increases in personal and organizational productivity. The Kanes' revolutionary time and project management technology will eliminate stress and feeling "overwhelmed" will become a thing of the past.

TRANSFORMATION IN THE WORKPLACE: A COMMUNICATION SEMINAR

This seminar provides an environment in which participants can explore various aspects of their communications and behavior and the impact they may unknowingly have on others in their work environment. In a loosely structured format, designed to allow one to discover the nuances of true communication, this course acts as a non-judgmental laboratory environment which reveals and dissolves those unaware, reflexive behaviors that are counter-productive in an office environment. Transformation in the Workplace is appropriate for people of all professions and is specifically geared towards those companies and individuals who want to operate at peak efficiency and who desire to have work be a highly satisfying experience.

Some of the areas in which previous participants have reported dramatic results:

• An increased ability to listen to clients and respond to their needs.
• Increased productivity
• Increased sales
• Greater job satisfaction
• Greater rapport with managers, co-workers and/or staff
• Less job related stress
• Fewer sick days
• Greater ease in dealing with "Problem" situations

INSTANTANEOUS TRANSFORMATION® WEEKENDS

In this exciting in-depth exploration, participants will have the opportunity to have a direct experience of Instantaneous Transformation®. Rather than teach techniques, the Kanes empower participants to get into the moment and reclaim their natural ability to access this state at will.

This workshop is designed to reveal and dissolve the mechanical behaviors and barriers which limit our lives and keep us stuck in our memories of the past or our plans for the future. In this course, participants can discover fulfillment in their lives without working on their "problems". Through light and playful exercises and group discussions the Kanes act as catalytic agents in facilitating people's discovery of their own truths.

At the end of the workshop participants bring home a deeper awareness, an expanded sense of self, a heightened sense of self worth, a less stressful attitude toward previously distressing situations, and a strengthened ability to be present in the moment— regardless of the circumstances. As a result, they discover a more honest, true and natural way of being that allows them to be increasingly effective, and satisfied, in all aspects of their lives.

THE ART OF BEING A HEALER

All of us are healers. Regardless of our roles in life, or our vocations, we all have the ability to heal ourselves and to be a healing presence for those around us. This course is not about learning another technique. It is about discovering the healer that dwells within each of us so that we can access that place at will. Participants discover the possibility of healing themselves and others with a beauty and simplicity that far surpasses what we generally think of healing to be.

THE FREEDOM TO BREATHE

This course is designed for people who want to dissolve the unconscious restrictions which limit their lives. Using breath as a tool, it is a gentle entry into the moment which can release past trauma, both emotional and physical, and result in a dramatically expanded sense of oneself.

THE ART OF RELATING

Imagine what it would be like to be able to relate well, day in and day out, not just when the circumstances happen to be easy. The Kanes have discovered the secrets to having relationships be fresh, loving and alive. After more than 15 years of marriage, people still ask them if they are newlyweds. Ariel and Shya invite you to join them as they share the key elements that bring relationships out of the realm of the ordinary and mundane and into the realm of the miraculous. This workshop will empower you to have nurturing and fulfilling relationships in all areas of your life. In the Art of Relating, you will rediscover your ability to create intimate, exciting profound relationships - including the one with yourself.

EXECUTIVE COACHING:

Individual coaching is available for those executives interested in achieving revolutionary increases in productivity, income, rapport and job satisfaction.

SEMINARS FOR COMPANIES:

The Kanes tailor private seminars to meet the needs of individual organizations or departments.

PRIVATE SESSIONS:

The Kanes meet with individuals and couples in person and by phone. They also offer individual healing sessions using Shya's revolutionary form of bodywork and pain relief, which was the forerunner to their Instantaneous Transformation® technology.

SEMINARS IN YOUR AREA...

If you want to be on the Kanes' mailing list or, want to know their current schedule of events, check their website at:

> http://www.ask-inc.com

or write to them at:

> ASK Productions, Inc.
> PMB 137
> 208 E. 51st Street
> New York, NY 10022-6500

If there is not an event scheduled in your area and you are interested in having Instantaneous Transformation® where you live and work, contact the Kanes... they listen.

WHAT PEOPLE ARE SAYING ABOUT THE KANES' SEMINARS AND CONSULTING SESSIONS

"When originally approached about doing an article about the Kanes' and their work, I told their friend about how many friends of teachers, gurus, facilitators, therapists, etc. with the newest approach or the heaviest credentials, had come knocking at my door offering nirvana and available time for an interview. I was not interested. I don't recall what opened my mind. I had been in therapy for most of the year and had felt frustrated that such a commitment of time and money and self-exploration had produced very limited results. The idea of jumping into another process seemed pointless. But, I decided to attend one of their evening gatherings anyway. I didn't know it then, but I was at the beginning of the end of years of working on myself.

A lot of time has come and gone since then. I know I have found something there that is very precious to me. Fresh air is what comes to mind. Complete love is what my heart says."
Paul English, Publisher, Managing Editor
Free Spirit Magazine

"Since working with the Kanes, I have experienced a 100% increase in my income while working 30% fewer hours. I work more efficiently because I listen effectively and act proactively. I no longer treat interruptions in my day as problems."
Robert Finnen, Computer Software Consultant

"At the end of my first workshop with Ariel and Shya Kane, I remember saying, "Nothing has happened, but everything has changed!" Within two months, I had quit my job, moved to New York and was living with a wonderful man to whom I am now happily married. These changes came about with virtually no effort on my part, they happened almost magically. There were no decisions made, no major goals set, no plots and plans — my life simply began to unfold."
Mary Yeager, Sales
Stock Exchange

"I met Ariel and Shya Kane at a low point in my life. At that time, I was 47 years old and unemployed. I had been downsized from my marketing management position with a company that I had been with for ten years.

I started taking the Kanes' transformational workshops and began feeling the importance of every moment. I discovered that by going full tilt in everything that was placed in front of me, my life became significantly more rewarding.

Then, while continuing to take seminars and workshops with the Kanes, I was hired by Staples Direct as an outside sales representative.

My results since joining Staples have been miraculous! In 1993 I was named National Rookie of the Year, and in 1994 through 1996 I was number one in dollar sales and new account acquisition across the United States. And now, I have been promoted to Regional Sales Manager for the Northeast.

I can say without any reservations that the joy and success in my life today both at work and with my new wife, could not have been accomplished without the Kanes' guidance. Before I met them, I would not have dreamed that my life could be so magical."

George R. Slatin
Regional Sales Manager for the Northeast
Staples Direct

"I highly recommend the Kanes' Transformation in the Workplace Seminar to anybody wishing to dramatically improve their performance and job satisfaction. After the workshop my ability to listen radically changed. It was as though a new, improved pair of ears had been fitted on me overnight!

As the Personal Assistant to the Director of the United Nations International School, I deal with a lot of people. One of the reasons I wanted to attend the workshop was that I felt I needed guidance in handling situations with people I would call "problematic" and with those who have abrasive personalities. I am so grateful that the school gave me the opportunity to attend the seminar and experience the Kanes' transformational technology.

I am now able to respond appropriately to others even in tense or confrontational situations. As a result I am much more effective in my role as a representative of the United Nations International School."

> *Isabelle Soudrie*
> *Personal Assistant to the Director*
> *United Nations International School*

"Ariel and Shya's weekly evening sessions are always a surprise and pleasure for me. Each time I go to one, there is a unique opportunity to discover who I am in that moment, and it is often not who I had expected. The particular magic that happens when this group of people comes together makes it easier and easier to pull myself out of my thoughts, worries, and my perceptions of who I think I am when I walk in the door. What I have discovered is that people truly love me."

> *Tom Maher, Vice President*
> *A major Wall Street Investment Bank*

"Josh first met Ariel and Shya Kane in May of 1988 at an evening seminar they were leading. We were not yet married. He came home full of excitement and enthusiasm. He said that he had just met the most incredible couple; they were full of life and in love, and I just had to meet them. We didn't realize then that our lives were about to transform and we can't remember how it happened. All we know is that after being around the Kanes, we have an extraordinary marriage, thriving practices and a great daughter. Life is pure magic."

> *Josh Blau, CPA*
> *Laura Blau, Esq.*

"Before my executive consulting session, I just wanted the days to be over already. I spent a lot of time justifying why I put off projects. I was not particularly productive. I felt sorry for myself, had no energy, I disliked everybody around me and avoided communications as much as possible.

Having had a session with the Kanes, my outlook totally shifted. My work flows easily, I have finished projects that previously seemed too daunting or cumbersome to even start. I appreciate talking to my customers and colleagues, I find everybody extremely cooperative and I handle whatever comes up without hesitation or procrastination. In summary: I get a lot done and I thoroughly enjoy my job. My thanks to Ariel and Shya!"

Stephanie Finnen
Vice President, NORD/LB

"It is difficult to find the words to succinctly yet sufficiently endorse the work of two people who have contributed so positively to my personal and professional growth, but endorse them I will and without qualification.

I can't exactly explain how it happened, but, since I have been attending their seminars and working with the Kanes in a "coaching relationship", my ability to work with people in all situations has dramatically improved, my department is stronger than ever, my responsibilities and income have continued to increase and I and my family have never been happier. The Kanes' wisdom, focus and insight have really paid off! It's available for you, too. I suggest you go for it."

Johnnie M. Jackson
Vice President, General Counsel and
Corporate Secretary, Olin Corporation